Introduction to Integrating
Music, Art, and Theatre
-in-
Elementary Education

Third Edition

Allison Manville Metz | Beth Gibbs | Hsiao-ping Chen

Kendall Hunt
publishing company

Cover image © Shutterstock.com

Kendall Hunt
publishing company

www.kendallhunt.com

Send all inquiries to:

4050 Westmark Drive

Dubuque, IA 52004-1840

CONTENTS

ACKNOWLEDGMENTS

The authors of this text would like to thank the following people for their help and support during the writing process:

Bob Largent and Michelle Bahr from Kendall Hunt
Patricia Gordon for her contributions in music
Bridget Kiger Lee
Cheryl Kaplan Zachariah
Claire Marie von Hirdler
Erika Hughes
Francesca Amari-Sajtar
Katheryn Phillips Bilbo
Kelly Bremner
Malinda Petersen
Mark Metz
Michelle Ebert Freire
Nick Bailey
Rachel Anderson
Ryan Kent Manville
Talleri McRae

&

Special thanks to our friends and families for their constant encouragement.

THE AUTHORS

Allison Manville Metz is Assistant Professor of Theatre Education at Grand Valley State University in Allendale, Michigan. "Dr. Alli" holds a Ph.D. in Theatre Research from The University of Wisconsin–Madison, as well as an M.F.A. in Drama and Theatre for Youth from The University of Texas–Austin. She is a proud member of the American Alliance for Theatre and Education (AATE) and was AATE's 2004 Winifred Ward Scholarship Award recipient. This is her first book, which she completed thanks to the support of husband, Mark.

Hsiao-ping Chen received her Ph.D. in art education from The Ohio State University. Currently, she is an Associate Professor of Art Education at Grand Valley State Univrsity. In addition to supervising student teachers, she teaches courses about computer technology integration, K-12 studio practice, and digital creativity. Her research interests include computer technology, arts integration, assessment and curriculum development, creativity and artmaking, identity formation, and popular culture.

Beth Gibbs received her Ph.D. from The Pennsylvania State University. She is currently an Associate Professor of Music Education at Grand Valley State University where she teaches courses in music education. Her professional interests include research into effective music teaching practices, music learning interactions, and the assessment practices of elementary music teachers.

INTRODUCTION

CURRENT CHALLENGES AND OPPORTUNITIES IN ARTS INTEGRATION IN U.S. SCHOOLS

After U.S. President Barack Obama ran on an Arts Policy platform as part of his 2008 campaign, he set in motion an 18-month study to assess the problems and possibilities facing arts education in schools. By May 2011, the President's Committee on the Arts and Humanities (PCAH) was ready to suggest action items, after the committee established two operational assumptions:

First, the arts are a vital part of the culture and life of this country, and all students deserve access to the arts in school as part of a complete education. Just as science and social studies are deemed essential subjects independent of their value to other learning outcomes, arts merit a similar unambiguous place in the curriculum. Second, decades of research and experience show that high quality arts education can play an important part in achieving a range of educational objectives. The arts can motivate and engage students; stimulate curiosity and foster creativity; teach 21st century skills such as problem solving and team work; and facilitate school-wide collaborations. While there is certainly room for additional information in these areas, there is no doubt that research about the value of arts education is positive and consistent.[1]

The PCAH went on to recommend that stakeholders in arts education employ the following five actions:

1. Build collaborations among different approaches.
2. Develop the field of arts integration.
3. Expand in-school opportunities for teaching artists.
4. Utilize federal and state policies to reinforce the place of arts in K-12 education.
5. Widen the focus of evidence gathering about arts education.

The results of the study reaffirmed and solidified what advocates for arts integration have always known: The arts are a viable and valuable tool in the classroom.

In December 2015, the Elementary and Secondary Education Act (ESEA) was reauthorized. The reauthorization of ESEA, known as the Every Student Succeeds Act (ESSA), was an amendment to the Elementary and Secondary Education Act of 1965. With the 2015 amendment, states were granted more flexibility in how they could use federal funds for education. Additionally, ESSA

---

[1] President's Committee on the Arts and Humanities, "Reinvesting in Arts Education: Winning America's Future Through Creative Schools," May 2011, www.pcah.gov/sites/default/files/PCAH_Reinvesting_4web .pdf (accessed May 28, 2011).

included the arts alongside math and language arts as part of a well-rounded education. Because the arts were included in the ESSA's definition of a well-rounded education, they would be eligible for the same funding opportunities as other content areas. Given states' increased flexibility in providing accountability for and use of federal funding, this also would allow arts education advocates more opportunities to encourage states to fund arts education programs.[2]

FOUNDATIONAL THEORY

The arts reflect the human condition. They speak to us about where we have been, what is important to us now, and what may come in the future. We experience enjoyment, entertainment, socialization, ritual, and reflection through our engagement in the arts. However, beyond the aesthetic enjoyment of the arts, the practice of arts in education and arts integration is grounded upon educational foundations. A foundation based upon Constructivism has informed our thoughts on arts education and must be understood by readers in order for pre-service and classroom teachers to embrace the efficacy of arts integration.

- **Constructivism:** The constructivist epistemology proposes that there is no single truth because individual truths are dependent on unique sociocultural understandings. This theory proposes that knowledge is subjective and formed from within, as a result of a student's beliefs and experiences. Students must discover and construct knowledge for themselves within the learning environment. In a constructivist approach to education, students will study a topic from multiple perspectives within an integrated curriculum.[3] Readers should be aware of two very important figures who have contributed to ideas relative to the constructivist theory: John Dewey and Lev Vygotsky.

  John Dewey (1859–1952), one of America's most influential educational psychologists, contributed to the constructivist theory by coining the motto, "learning by doing." Dewey's experiential learning model continues to promote and influence real world applications within school curriculum. In Lev Vygotsky's constructivist perspective, called "sociocultural theory," social interactions help to stimulate developmental processes and cognitive growth, and learning and development cannot be separated from the context in which they occur. One of the key concepts of Vygotsky's social-cultural theory is the *zone of proximal development* (ZPD). When a student is in the ZPD, he or she is able to achieve more with assistance than he or she could do individually in his or her *zone of actual development* (ZAD). Vygotsky is also credited with solidifying the theory of "scaffolding," which, like construction scaffolding, uses instruction to support developing ideas before students can gain further understandings.[4]

GOALS OF THIS BOOK

This book is designed to serve as an introduction to the ways music, art, and theatre can be integrated into the elementary school curriculum. Sections on each of the three disciplines will include information specific to the arts' subject areas (for arts education purposes) as well as pedagogical techniques for use in the classroom (for arts integration). As a practical guide for both pre-service and current elementary teachers, we have included sample lesson plans, activities, discussion questions, and resource information.

---

[2] National Art Education Association, "ESEA Reauthorization is Finalized as Every Student Succeeds Act," May 2016, https://www.arteducators.org/advocacy/essa-every-student-succeeds-act (accessed May 11, 2016).

[3] Dale H. Schunk, *Learning Theories: An Educational Perspective* (Upper Saddle River, NJ: Pearson Education, 2004), 287.

[4] Schunk, *Learning Theories: An Educational Perspective*, 293–297.

DISCUSSION QUESTIONS

Discussion questions are included at the end of each section to allow the reader to reflect on the goals of that particular section. Questions have been designed to either initiate classroom discussion, or use as writing assignments. The authors of this book would like to encourage readers to also incorporate personal experiences when justifying their answers in order to integrate their established knowledge of real-world events with new concepts they are reading about in this text.

1. The PCAH summary report mentioned several challenges America's schools are currently facing. Have you experienced any of these challenges in your own schooling? How do you think these challenges will affect you as a teacher?
2. Of the five recommendations mentioned in the summary report, which do you feel able to contribute to in the future? How do you see creating opportunities for arts integration in your classroom?
3. The Every Student Succeeds Act includes arts education as part of a well-rounded education. How would you describe a well-rounded education?
4. What questions do you have right now about the constructivist approach to learning?

ART, THEATER, AND MUSIC IN SPECIAL EDUCATION

by **Mary Clancy**

In teaching students with disabilities, educators are often presented with numerous challenges in terms of lesson planning, implementation, and assessment for students with a wide range of needs, not to mention the daily challenge of engaging students with alternative learning styles for seven hours a day! Some of the most difficult challenges for a classroom teacher come from finding ways to engage all types of learners at once. Theater, art, and movement activities provide opportunities for students to apply knowledge in new ways, engage with material in collaborative environments, and quite frankly, just get up out of their seats! According to social constructivist theorists, learning does not take place in isolation; instead, it is a collaborative process that places the learner in an active role (Brooks & Brooks, 1999). Obviously, all of these ideas can be easier said than done. As a classroom teacher, it is not impossible to plan drama, music, and art activities for students with special needs. Here are some tips to keep in mind as you consider art, theater, and music activities in your own classrooms.

1. THINK CAREFULLY ABOUT STUDENT GROUPINGS
   Group work and cooperative learning settings have been shown to promote increased levels of achievement, more time on task, higher levels of self-esteem, and more opportunities for positive cooperation among students (Slavin, 1990). However, if you have a class of students with a wide range of needs, having students count off into four groups is not likely going to be the best way to maximize participation and success. When planning your lesson or activity, think carefully about the groups. Which students need more support? Who has strengths in language and who needs clear models? Who is able to work independently? Which students work well together? Collaborative activities often provide students with authentic opportunities to construct knowledge together. Think about students who have different strengths and different areas to shine when arranging groups. Choose students who will have opportunities to learn from each other.

2. USE A GRADUAL RELEASE OF RESPONSIBILITY MODEL WHEN INTRODUCING NEW ACTIVITIES
   Think about riding a bike. It likely occurred as a series of events in which you gradually took over more responsibility for the task. First you watched someone riding a bike (the teacher has complete control); then someone showed you how by walking alongside you and holding onto the handlebars (the teacher and student share responsibility); as a third step, maybe someone stood at the end of your driveway and gave you encouragement and shouted out some tips (the teacher guides the student); and then finally one day you were able to shout at the door that you were going for a bike ride and you'd be back in a little while (student is independent). It is good practice to follow a similar gradual release of responsibility (Pearson & Gallagher, 1983) when introducing a new activity and teaching a new skill to students. Show students what you expect them to do, guide them through it by creating a shared experience, and then eventually they will be independent.

3. REPEAT, REPEAT, REPEAT
   Students with disabilities need repetition and review in order for new skills to become an internal process. Consider using just one activity over a week, a month, or even an entire

unit. As activities become a routine, students will be able to engage in them consistently and with increased independence.

4. SCAFFOLD AND PROVIDE OPPORTUNITIES FOR EXTERNAL ORGANIZATION
Drama activities require multiple steps and asking students to apply knowledge in ways that require higher-level processes. For students with disabilities, this can be a lot to manage and organize. Use graphic organizers to allow students time to plan for each step of the activity in a manageable way. For example, if you asking students to think of an action that represents a character's emotion, a simple t-chart might help students access this content work.

Character Feeling	Action
- the character felt nervous on the first day of school	-make a sad face and cover my eyes

5. THINK SMALL
When planning an art, music, or theater activity for students with disabilities, think small. Break down each activity into a manageable chunk and give your students time to work with each new expectation. This might mean that one new activity will take a week to complete; that's okay! Set reasonable goals and guide students through each step of the way.

Teaching students with vast ranges of needs in one classroom is a daunting task. Art, drama, and music activities can be valuable tools in working with diverse populations; but incorporating activities that are loud and messy can be overwhelming. Ultimately, when done carefully and purposefully, there are ways to reach all types of learners and create opportunities for successful access to the curriculum. Don't be afraid to try new things and remember to take it one step at time. Remember that not everything is going to work for you, just like not everything is going to work for your students. Reflect on successes and revise what didn't work. There's always tomorrow to try again.

THREE SAMPLE MODIFICATIONS FOR A DRAMA ACTIVITY: BEFORE, DURING, AND AFTER

Activity: Tableau

"Pre-Activity" Modification 1
    If introducing a tableau activity for the first time, consider having students create still-scenes of a photograph before asking them to create an independent scene. The photograph will introduce them to the idea that their bodies can represent abstract concepts and that they are able to use motions and poses to demonstrate a "larger idea." Carefully choose a photograph that has accessible ideas and concrete ideas. Facial expressions and body language are easier to unpack than abstract ideas like "friendship" or "change in character." You may also consider photographing a tableau that students perform and using it in subsequent lessons connecting to the curriculum. The repetition and personal connection to student experience is beneficial for students with disabilities.

During-Activity: Modification 2
Instead of explaining the activity to students and then having them break into groups to work on their own, break down the activity into single-step directions and processes. A supporting worksheet for each group will guide students through the multi-step process and allow for students with disabilities to access the activity in a clear and tangible manner. A guiding worksheet should include explicit directions for each step of the process.

Name_____   Date_____

PLANNING FOR YOUR SCENE

1. Choose the scene you would like to represent: _____

2. Discuss with your group:

   What are the key ideas in the scene? How are you going to represent them?

Idea	Why is it important?	How can we represent it in our tableau?

3. Make a plan with your group of your responsibilities.

Name	What are you going to do in the scene?

3. Practice your scene with the group.

   How did it go? Do you need to make changes to your responsibilities?

4. Practice your scene one more time and get ready to share with the class.

Post-Activity: Modification 3

It is important to provide students with opportunities to reflect and process what they learned in multiple formats. For many students, especially those with language-based disabilities, a whole-group discussion may not be the most accurate way of assessing understanding. Consider giving students a "choice" period after drama activities with various ways to demonstrate their understanding. For students with difficulties in social communication, it is likely they will need independent time after particularly collaborative activities that may have pushed their comfort zone. After an activity such as a tableau, try a center-based reflection time before processing the activity with the whole class. Students can sign up for an independent or group activity and the teacher is able to work individually with students who may need support in processing the lesson. In having a "pre-reflection" time, students will be more prepared to participate in a whole-group discussion of comprehension the following period or day.

Choice A	Choice B
Independent	Group Discussion
Write or draw in your journal about today's activity.	Talk with your group about today's activity. Have one person record your thoughts.
1. What did you like about the activity?/ What went well for you?	1. What did you like about the activity? What went well for you?
2. What did you learn about the characters in our book?	2. What did you learn about the characters in our book?

Author bio

Mary Clancy's professional career has centered on creating appropriate and effective educational environments for students with disabilities, specifically in urban environments. She has studied Special Education and Literacy Education at New York University and the City College of New York and has been a classroom teacher of students with disabilities in both public and private schools for 10 years. Mary is currently the Division Head at the Cooke Center Academy, a school for students with cognitive and developmental disabilities in New York City.

REFERENCES

Brooks, J., & Brooks, M. (1999). *In search of understanding: The case for the constructivist classroom.* Alexandria, VA: ASCD.

Pearson, P. D., & Gallagher, M. D. (1983). The instruction of reading comprehension. *Contemporary Educational Psychology, 8*, 317–344.

Slavin, R. (1990). *Cooperative learning: Theory, research, and practice.* Englewood, NJ: Prentice Hall.

CHAPTER 1

◇◇◇◇◇◇◇◇◇◇◇◇◇◇

MUSIC

WHY MUSIC?

The Meaning of Music in our Lives and Schools

Music is a daily presence in our lives. In many ways, we engage in musical experiences without conscious thought: We awake to music on our radios, we hear and see music on television, we sing along to our favorite songs in the car on our way to school and work, and we feel compelled to move and dance to music. How has music become so present in our daily experiences? As social beings, we have a desire to share our life experiences with others, and music often allows us to express what words alone cannot. There is power in the shared human experience of music to make us feel. It can inspire us to laugh and rejoice or cry and feel sorrow. Music triggers remembrances of past times, places, experiences, and people. It has the power to unite us with shared experience and to provide us with cultural identity.

What is the meaning of music? According to ethnomusicologist Christopher Small[1], music is not a thing, but an activity. It is something people do. As such, the meaning of music in our lives lies within the individual meanings we bring to our active experiences through listening to or creating music. The ways in which people experience music in their lives vary. Music makers can be individuals or groups, amateurs and professionals, those who perform for others, and those who perform for personal enjoyment. When we listen to music, sometimes we do this socially and at other times we listen alone. The different ways we experience and express ourselves musically speak to the musical contexts in which we live[2].

Philosophical Perspectives in Music Education

The values we bring to music can be expressed in terms of individual experience or through the shared values of community and culture. The value of music within our schools is relative to the value and meaning we hold for music in our lives. From a philosophical perspective, music education is tied to the function of music in the lives of children. In the aesthetic approach to music

---

[1] Christopher Small, *Musicking: The Meanings of Performers and Listening* (Middletown: Wesleyan University Press, 1998), 2–3.

[2] Bonnie Wade, *Thinking Musically: Experiencing Music, Expressing Culture* (New York: Oxford University Press, 2004), 1–2.

education, most strongly associated with Bennett Reimer, aesthetic education in music attempts to enhance learning in the following ways:

1. Musical sounds (as various cultures construe what these are) create and share meaning available only from such sounds.
2. Creating musical meanings, and partaking of them, requires an amalgam of mind, body, and feeling.
3. Musical meanings incorporate within them a great variety of universal/cultural/individual meanings (ideas, beliefs, values, associations, etc.) transformed by musical sounds.
4. Gaining its special meanings requires direct experience with musical sounds, deepened and expanded by skills, knowledge, understandings, attitudes, and sensitivities education can cultivate.[3]

In this view, music is of value to us and our children for the unique, inherent, and individual meanings derived from participating in the art form. A different philosophical perspective is offered by David Elliot. In his praxial philosophy, music learning takes place through active participation in the art. "Musical experiences are valued in practical terms. Music makers and listeners achieve self-growth, self-knowledge, and enjoyment in the constructive actions of musicing and listening."[4] The praxial philosophy places more emphasis on the meanings derived from actively creating music and the context in which music is being created. Despite differing perspectives on how musical meaning is generated, I suggest that both offer a valid view on the ways in which we engage with music and how we can provide meaningful musical experiences for our students. Music education allows our students the opportunity to create meanings and experience feelingful responses to the sounds they experience by actively participating through creating, performing, and responding to music. Furthermore, all humans have musical aptitude. Just as we have potential to achieve success in different academic areas such and language and math, we have the potential to achieve musically. If we do not nurture this aptitude within our students through musical experiences, we deprive them of the means to reach their full potential to experience music in a meaningful way.

National Core Arts Standards

The National Coalition for Core Arts Standards has developed a set of national standards for dance, media arts, music, theatre, and visual arts. These standards are voluntary guidelines for what students should know and be able to do. The eleven anchor standards are categorized under four types of artistic processes: creating, performing, responding, and connecting. The standards for music education provide specific guidelines for what students should be able to accomplish musically at different grade levels.

By providing our students with opportunities to engage in musical experiences as outlined in the core standards, we can help to better nurture their potential to understand the music around them, to create and respond to music in meaningful ways, to critically evaluate music and musical experiences, and to make connections which allow them to understand music within the context of society and culture.[5]

---

[3] Bennett Reimer, *A Philosophy of Music Education: Advancing the Vision* (Upper Saddle River: Pearson Education, Inc., 2003), 11.

[4] David Elliot, *Music Matters: A New Philosophy of Music Education* (New York: Oxford University Press, 1995), 124.

[5] The National Coalition for Core Arts Standards, "National Core Arts Standards", accessed May 11, 2016, http://www.nationalartsstandards.org/

Utilitarian Values of Music Education

Beyond the inherent value of learning music as an expressive art, students may benefit from music in a variety of other ways. When music or music education is used to help achieve an extra-musical purpose, it is given utilitarian value. For example, a teacher might use a song to help students remember the names of the states and their capitals. Memorization is just one way in which music can be used to help students learn. A teacher could also use music to introduce students to the beliefs and practices of a culture they may be learning about. Furthermore, music may positively enhance various cognitive and physiological processes in the body. Eric Jensen, author of *Arts with the Brain in Mind*, makes a case for the inclusion of music in school curricula through the following arguments:

1. Music enhances our biological survival.
2. It has predictable developmental periods.
3. Cognitive systems are enhanced, including visual-spatial, analytical, mathematical, and creative.
4. Emotional systems are positively affected, including endocrine, hormonal, social, personal skills, cultural, and aesthetic appreciation.
5. Perceptual-motor systems are enhanced, including listening, vestibular systems, sensory acuity, timing, and state management.
6. Stress response system is enhanced, which includes the immune response and autonomic nervous system, the sympathetic and parasympathetic systems.
7. Memory systems are activated through improved listening, attention, concentration and recall.[6]

Given that most schools provide limited time for music instruction each week, students may not receive the full benefits of exposure to music unless teachers make a conscious effort to support the consistent use of music throughout the curriculum.

[6] Eric Jensen, *Art with the Brain in Mind* (Alexandria: ASCD, 2001), 14.

Name: _____

DISCUSSION QUESTIONS

1. What musical experiences do you remember from your childhood?

2. What types of musical experiences do you remember from school?

3. In what ways do you most often engage in musical experiences?

4. Do you have a favorite piece of music or an artist you prefer to listen to? What about that music speaks to you?

5. Consider the following ways in which music is typically used in elementary classrooms. For each, describe an example of an experience you had in which a teacher used this strategy and explain how this would benefit students. If you are unable to recall a specific example from your personal experience, explain how you as a teacher could use this technique in the future.
    a. Teaching a song to reinforce an academic concept
    b. Using music to provide cultural or historical context to a unit
    c. Playing music to calm the class or aid creative endeavors

THE MUSICAL NATURE OF STUDENTS

Human beings are musical beings. We create, perform, and respond to music because it helps us to communicate in a feelingful way. We enjoy listening to a wide variety of musical genres and create preferences for the types of music that speak to us as individuals. Many people enjoy performing musically, either as professionals or amateurs, and find fulfillment in the physical expression of music for their own enjoyment and the enjoyment of others who listen to them. Whether performing live or attending a live concert, a connection is formed between the performers and the audience. Other people create music through composition, improvisation, or arrangement to express new musical ideas and interpretations. In essence, music is a part of us whether we create, perform, or respond to music, and would not exist as prevalently throughout our culture today and in the past if we did not derive meaning and enjoyment from it.

Learning to engage with others musically can benefit students artistically, socially, kinesthetically, academically, and can be presented to students in a variety of ways. Visual learners can be engaged through the use of listening guides that can visually represent different aspects of musical experiences. Auditory learners can engage in the aural expression of music through listening to different songs and musical recordings in the classroom. Kinesthetic learners can move to music in the classroom, embodying different elements of musical expression. A variety of musical experiences in which students can visualize, listen to, and move to music, will benefit the different types of learners in the classroom.

When we plan for lessons to creatively engage our students' minds and bodies, we must keep in mind the multiple ways they learn and the individual differences which make students unique. A "one size fits all" approach to instruction is inadvisable because techniques that work for one child may not work as well for another. It is also important to recognize that our students have different strengths and potentials in the academic and artistic disciplines offered as part of the school curriculum. By providing a wide variety of opportunities and contexts for students to engage in learning, we can help to nurture their individual strengths while offering a well-rounded environment for learning.

Audiation

Renowned researcher and professor of music education Edwin Gordon has coined the term *audiation* as "the ability to hear and to understand music for which the sound is not physically present or may never have been physically present."[7] For example, think of the tune to "Mary Had a Little Lamb." Even if you forget the words, think through melody at least once. Now, can you think of the same tune slower . . . faster . . . with a higher starting pitch . . . in minor mode instead of major? This tune you've been thinking about and manipulating is not physically present, but you are able to audiate, or think it. Can you understand what you changed to create different variations of the tune in your musical mindscape? Part of audiation is being able to understand the context of music. Is the tune moving in twos or threes? Where is the strong beat? Can you identify the resting tone of the tune?

When we listen to someone speak, when we converse with others, read, and write, we do so within the context of a language bound by grammar, syntax, and semantics. Our ability to understand the context of the language we are using is essential to ensuring good communication. Similarly, when we audiate or create/perform/respond to music in some way, we do so within a musical context that allows us to understand the music in some way and anticipate what may come next. These musical contexts, which will be explored in the next section of this book, help to provide a basis for comprehension of musical ideas.

---

[7] Edwin E. Gordon, *Preparatory Audiation, Audiation, and Music Learning Theory: A Handbook of a Comprehensive Music Learning Sequence* (Chicago: GIA Publications, Inc., 2001), 3.

Musical Aptitude

As mentioned previously, the students in our classes have different academic and artistic strengths. The potential to learn in a specific area is called an aptitude. Aptitude differs from achievement: The former indicates potential to learn, whereas the latter refers to what has already been learned. Musical aptitude is a student's potential to learn music. A student with high musical aptitude might also demonstrate a high level of musical achievement, but this is not always the case. A student with lower musical aptitude could achieve more than a student with a high musical aptitude given enough motivation and effort. Edwin Gordon, who has studied musical aptitude in great detail, suggests the following:

> A child is born with a particular level of music aptitude. That level changes in accordance with the quality of the child's informal and formal music environment until the child is approximately nine years old. Thus, neither nature nor nurture is solely responsible for the child's level of musical aptitude.[8]

Given the flexible nature of children's musical aptitude, classroom teachers can help to nurture students' potential to learn musically, enriching their musical environments by providing a variety of musical experiences in the classroom. Furthermore, it is important to recognize that all children have musical aptitude, and classroom musical experiences may give children the opportunity to achieve in music when they might struggle in other academic areas.

The Development of Children's Singing Voices

Just as musical aptitude will vary among students, so will their use of appropriate singing voices. Many times, a student who is perceived of as tone-deaf or as a non-singer simply hasn't learned to sing in the appropriate register. The same can be true of adults. The majority of time we use our voices to speak, we are using the lower end of our vocal register. Sometimes this lower register is referred to as the chest voice. Singing in the lower range will only allow students to access a narrow range of pitches, and they may feel vocal strain by singing in this register. When we sing appropriately, we use not only the lower register, but a lighter middle and upper (head) registers as well. Before working on vocal development, it is important to assess how students are currently using their voices. The following categories, developed by Joanne Rutkowski indicate different vocal ranges or stages you may encounter in your students' voices.

> *Pre-singer*: Often referred to as a non-singer, this child, when asked to sing, chants the words to a song instead.
> *Speaking Range Singer*: This child sings, but in his or her speaking voice (low) register. This register is from about A3 to C4 for young children but begins to expand upwards in pitch as the child enters the middle and upper elementary school grades.
> *Limited Range Singer*: This stage is exhibited by some children in the primary grades. The middle register (a lighter quality of voice) is used when singing, but the range of this voice is very narrow, usually D3 to F-sharp4. Some middle and upper elementary school children will exhibit this register, but many will sing in this range with their speaking (low) register.
> *Initial Range Singer*: This child uses the middle register and sings with a range from D4 to A4, often referred to as initial song range. A register lift in the voice occurs from A4 to B4-flat (from middle to upper register). These students do not access the upper register yet. The teacher

---

[8] Gordon, *Preparatory Audiation, Audiation, and Music Learning Theory*, 81.

should listen carefully for the quality of voice that students use when singing in the initial song range. Upper elementary students can access this range with their speaking (low) register. *Singer*: This child does lift the voice above the register lift and uses the upper (head) register.[9]

For children who are unused to using the middle and upper parts of their vocal range, simple vocal exercises may be used to help them access their full vocal range. The following exercises may be helpful in getting students to use lighter voices and a broader singing range.

1. Breathing is important to proper vocal production. Imagine sipping air through a straw. Allow the air to expand first the abdomen, then the ribs while keeping shoulders down and relaxed.
2. Vocal sirens allow students to experiment with the entirety of their vocal range. Have students imitate a police, ambulance, or fire siren. Trace the shape of the siren in the air for students to follow: lower for lower pitches, and higher for higher pitches. Vary the siren in a variety of ways. Allow students the opportunity to lead others in siren exercises.
3. Animal sound echoes allow students to use their voices in a variety of ways. Storybooks with different animals can be used with younger students as they identify the animals and recreate their sounds. Some children's songs, such as "Old MacDonald," also allow opportunities for students to improvise on animal vocal sounds.
4. Tossing a scarf into the air, students can mimic the slow floating descent of the scarf to the ground with their voices. You can also limit how low the scarf is allowed to drop before they must toss it in the air again.
5. In pairs, students may gently toss beanbags and vocally mimic the arch of the beanbag through the air until their partner catches it.
6. Simple echo microphones, which can often be bought for a dollar at discount stores, allow students to hear what they sound like and whether it matches the teacher's vocal model. Echo songs or call and response songs, such as "Charlie Over the Ocean," are great to use with echo microphones because students have the opportunity to hear the vocal prompt and sing their response.
7. The game "Simon Says" can be altered to "Simon Sings" where students are only allowed to perform the motions indicated when the prompts are sung. Students may take turns as the leader in this game.
8. Visualization techniques may also be useful. Have students image that they are swimming just below the surface of the ocean or a lake. That is their speaking voice. Then, have the students imagine they are drifting on the air currents just above the water. That is their singing voice.

As a general recommendation, the more opportunities students have to sing in class, the more comfortable they will become with their singing voices. Children should never be told to "mouth the words" to songs. Instead, positive encouragement and patience should be used to get them to produce appropriate light singing voices. Also keep in mind that students will be more likely to enjoy using their voices to sing when the teacher supplies an appropriate and positive vocal model. Don't hesitate to use the exercises mentioned to become more comfortable with your own singing voice.

[9] Joanne Rutkowski and Maria Runfola, *TIPS: The Child Voice* (Reston, VA: MENC, 1997), 3–4.

Name: _____

DISCUSSION QUESTIONS

1. Can you identify an example of a time when you were consciously or subconsciously audiating?

2. What are some elements of musical context that help us to understand the music that we audiate?

3. In what ways do students differ?

4. What types of classroom experiences could help to nurture students' musical aptitude?

5. What do you remember about your experiences singing in class when you were in elementary school?

6. How do you feel about your own singing voice?

MUSICAL CONTEXTS

Our interactions with music occur in a variety of ways and in a multitude of contexts. For most of us, we passively experience the music in our environment that comes from the radio, our mp3 players, or television. It is also common to interact with music in our environment by singing along with familiar lyrics and moving to the beat that we feel. Music does not need to be physically present for us to engage in musical behaviors, as anyone who has had a catchy commercial jingle stuck in their head can attest. We might even hum along or whistle a tune that has been on our minds. In school, we can help to facilitate a variety of interactions with music to engage students. In this section, we will explore different musical contexts in which elementary students can experience and actively participate in music making.

Creating Music

Whenever we engage students in a writing activity, we ask them to create through composition. When we speak and hold conversation, we improvise to convey our meanings. These actions come naturally to us through speech. Musical creation through composition, arrangement, and improvisation can initially be daunting to teachers or students who don't converse in the language of music with the same frequency as speech. Simple steps can be taken, however, to help facilitate student and teacher musical creativity. The following activities are basic ways to begin engaging students in creative musical thinking and expression. After each example, space is allotted for you to fill in your own ideas and examples.

Title of Activity: Rhythm Conversation Improvisation

- Objective: Students will be able to improvise basic duple and triple rhythm patterns through call and response.
- Target grade: K-5–Patterns may increase in complexity with grade and ability level.
- Number of participants: This will begin as a whole class activity. Students will later be in pairs.
- Room arrangement: Normal seating arrangements are fine.
- Materials (if any): None for basic version.
- Description of the activity: Beginning with the whole class, the teacher will clap several simple duple or triple rhythm patterns for students to echo. Each pattern should be 4 macro beats long. Next, the teacher will ask students to respond with a different clapping pattern. (Some students will still echo the teacher. This is okay and should lessen with practice.) After the class has had practice responding with different patterns, the teacher may ask for responses from small groups, and then finally individuals. Next, students will be paired. One student will be the "call" and the other student will be the "response." Given a steady tempo set by the teacher, pairs will engage in rhythmic dialogues, changing and creating new call and response patterns.
- Variations: Add other body percussion to clapping because this will allow for greater variety in pattern creation. Use classroom instruments or drums if available, or have students create their own instruments using found objects to play patterns.
- Adaptation for students with special needs: content of rhythm patterns may be either simplified or enhanced in complexity or duration. For students who struggle to create a unique response pattern, a sample bank of acceptable rhythmic responses may be created for their reference.

Title of Activity: Soundscape Composition

- Objective: Students will re-create, arrange, and perform the sounds of a chosen environment or story.
- Target grade: 3-5.
- Number of participants: Whole class, small groups, or individuals.
- Room arrangement: Any.
- Materials (if any): Found objects or classroom instruments such as shakers, drums, bells, rainsticks, etc.
- Description of the activity: Beginning with a very basic story or nursery rhyme (such as Jack and Jill), the teacher will ask students to create the sounds to mimic the action of the story. After practicing the sounds as a class, students will perform as the teacher recites the story or rhyme. Next, the students will perform the sounds without narration. In small groups, students will be assigned or can choose different familiar stories to aurally illustrate in a similar way. After practicing, the small groups will perform for the class, allowing their peers to guess which story they were assigned (or had chosen). Audio recordings can be made of the performances. One week later, audio recordings can be played as students will try to recognize the soundscapes.
- Variations: Students may write their own stories and choose the appropriate sound effects to be performed by their classmates. In this version, the student becomes composer, arranger, conductor, and performer.
- Adaptation for students with special needs: Students needing assistance with the composition task are provided with peer support in the structure of this activity. Concrete tasks can be assigned to group members to help clarify procedures.

Title of Activity: Body Percussion Arrangement

- Objective: Students will arrange and perform a variety of rhythm patterns using body percussion.
- Target grade: 2-5–Patterns will increase in number and complexity with grade level and ability.
- Number of participants: Whole class.
- Room arrangement: Normal seating with space for students to stand and move in place.
- Materials (if any): Paper and pencils, whiteboard or projector.
- Description of the activity: As a class, the teacher and students will create at least three basic rhythm patterns as the basis for the arrangement. Patterns may be performed by clapping, tapping, patting, stomping, and snapping (or a mix). Each pattern will be associated with a different visual shape or letter. The class will practice performing each pattern individually when cued by the teacher pointing to the corresponding shape on the board. Next, the teacher will write a sequence of eight shapes or letters (they may repeat), which students will practice and perform in order. Next, students will create their own sequence of eight letters or shapes to be performed by the class. After practicing and performing individual student examples, multiple student arrangements can be layered on the board to be performed simultaneously or in sequence.
- Variations: Use of found objects or classroom instruments
- Adaptation for students with special needs: The length of the pattern sequence and the content of the rhythm patterns can be altered to reduce or enhance the complexity of the activity. Students may also work in pairs, rather than individually, to create their own sequence if peer assistance is helpful.

Name: _____

Practice: Write your own activity to engage students in musical creativity, arrangement, or improvisation.

Title of activity:

- Objective:

- Target grade:

- Number of participants:

- Room arrangement:

- Materials (if any):

- Source:

- Description of the activity:

- Variations:

Performing Music

Performing music through singing or playing instruments is a simple way to musically engage students in the classroom. As mentioned in the previous section on the nature of the student, children's voices may go through a variety of stages of vocal register development. By providing frequent opportunities for students to sing, they will become more comfortable using their singing voices. Providing positive performance opportunities for students in class reinforces vocal skill development and allows students to also practice good audience behavior. A variety of song genres may be used to engage students in singing including ballads, singing games, folk tunes, spirituals, blues, rounds, call and response songs, partner songs, as well as many others. I also encourage teachers to find and teach simple songs from different cultures and in different languages and to find songs with specific educational content that may align with another curricular lesson. The songs and sources listed in the References and Resources section on pages 43–45 may provide a starting place for teachers seeking song ideas.

Although musical performance in the elementary classroom may demonstrated most accessibly through singing, other means of performance are open to teachers who apply a little ingenuity. A lack of classroom instruments may provide teachers and students with the opportunity to use body percussion or create their own instruments to play. Additionally, chanting the words to poems or songs engages students in experience the metric pulse of speech rhythms.

Name: _____

PRACTICE

1. List the songs you remember performing in elementary school. Beside each song, indicate whether it was used to help reinforce a specific learning objective.

2. Plan and create your own unique instrument to use as an accompaniment to singing/chanting or to play as part of a drum circle. List all of the household materials or found objects you will need to create the instrument. Consider how the sound will be produced and whether you will be able to play the instrument in multiple ways. Also keep in mind the ability of elementary students to reproduce your instrument in the context of a classroom activity when designing your instrument.

Responding to Music

It is human nature to respond to the music in our environment. When using music in the classroom, response is integral to assessing how students perceive the music they hear. Responses to music can be fostered in a variety of ways through attentive listening, and movement. This section will outline ways to inspire student response to music.

Attentive listening: When playing recorded music in the classroom, we can assume that students hear the music, but we cannot know for certain if they are attentively listening to music unless we direct their listening in a specific way. The simplest way to do this is by asking guided listening questions. For example, if playing a recording or singing the traditional English lullaby, "The Riddle Song," you could ask students to listen think about possible to the riddles that occur in the first verse. Then, after hearing student answers, you could play or perform the rest of the song, which answers the riddles in the third verse.

<h2 style="text-align:center">The Riddle Song</h2>

I gave my love a cherry without a stone

I gave my love a chicken without a bone

I gave my love a ring that had no end

I gave my love a baby with no crying

How can there be a cherry that has no stone?

How can there be a chicken that has no bone?

How can there be a ring that has no end?

How can there be a baby with no crying?

A cherry when it's blooming it has no stone

A chicken when it's hatching, it has no bone

A ring while it's rolling, it has no end

A baby when it's sleeping, has no crying

Another way to guide listening is through the use of props or manipulatives. For examples, students could be given cards with different colors or shapes representing different aspects of music such as dynamics or tempo. Students would hold up the cards corresponding to what they hear in the musical example you play. Pipe cleaners are also good to use as a manipulative during student listening task. Upon playing a piece of music, students can manipulate the shape of the pipe cleaners to represent the melodic contour of the piece they are listening to.

Visual listening guides are also an excellent way to direct student attention during music listening. Listening guides can include lyrics, shapes, and/or images to represent the music. Students are able to follow the visual cues and track the changes in the musical example. For example, if you were to play the beginning phrases of Beethoven's 5th Symphony, a simple listening guide might look like this:

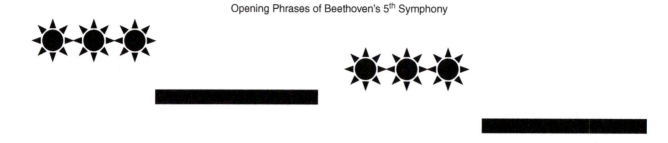

Opening Phrases of Beethoven's 5th Symphony

You can also have students create their own listening guides or listening maps to represent what they hear in the music. Ideally, they would be able to trade or share their listening guides with other students in the classroom to find out how well they were able to represent the music through visual cues. For students who may be visually impaired, consider using manipulatives such as blocks, strings, sticks, and scarves to create a tactile listening map. Listening guides designed by the teacher on poster board so that visually impaired students can trace the lines to follow along with the musical contour and other musical elements represented on the guide.

Name: _____

PRACTICE

1. Create a list of recordings you would consider using for an attentive listening activity:

2. Create a visual listening guide for one of the recordings you listed in activity 1 above.

Response through movement:

Movement is another technique to assess student response to music. Simple movement activities will allow students to respond to musical elements such as the rhythmic pulse or bear, tempo, meter, and form. Movement can be simple hand motions, whole body movement, structured dance, or movement using props such as parachutes or scarves.

Hand movements can be simple indications of tempo and meter or more varied patterns of motions to represent different musical phrases or specific lyrics. To engage your students in movement through hand motions, you can create your own version of a "Hand Jive" for students to learn and perform with any up-tempo recording. You will need to create a simple pattern of repeated hand motions for students to learn and repeat. I like to do movements in sets of eight. For example:

- Pat knees twice
- Clap twice
- Bump fists twice
- Bump fists again twice (switching top and bottom hands)
- Snap right twice
- Snap left twice
- Thumb over right shoulder twice
- Thumb over left shoulder twice
- REPEAT

For students with limited mobility, consider the range of movements you could incorporate into your sequence. You do not need to limit movements to hand motions. Think about using motions that can be performed while seated, using just the feet, using the face and shoulders, or using just the fingers.

Name: _____

PRACTICE

1. Create your own list of "hand-jive" movements

Whole body movements can be instigated through a simple game of "Follow the Leader." Standing in a circle, create simple movements to the beat for students to mimic. It is important to coordinate these movements with the beat of the recording you choose to use. Try to incorporate all body parts separately before adding motions using more than one body part at a time. When students are comfortable following your movements to the music, have them take turns leading the group in the game.

If you have space enough in your classroom, or available space close by outside or in a gymnasium, you can have students engage in locomotor movements across the space of the room. You can direct movements by asking students to move in a specific way around or across the room, have students generate ideas for different ways to move, or create specific rules for movement to account for changing musical elements. For example, if the music is playing quietly, I might ask students to use small motions or move close to the floor, whereas when the music is playing loudly I would ask them to create larger movements or to stand and move as tall as possible. As in the hand jive example, consider range of motion and alternate motions for students with limited mobility.

Props can also help to generate ideas for creative movement. Scarves can be used by individual students to show phrasing and movement of music. Small, six-person parachutes can be used have students nonverbally communicate and demonstrate visually what they hear in different musical examples. When using props, try to find musical examples with contrasting or changing material for a greater variety of possible movements from students.

STRATEGIES FOR USING MUSIC IN THE CLASSROOM

Co-authored by Patricia Gordon

Principles of Music Instruction

When engaging in musical experiences with your students, the following principles will help to facilitate student learning.

1. Sound before sight: Music should be presented aurally before students are given any iconic or visual reference.
2. Familiar before unfamiliar: Begin with what the students know. Children often engage in musical games and chants as they play. This can serve as a bridge to introducing new music that might have similar patterns of melody and rhythm. The familiar music becomes a basis for comparison with new repertoire that is introduced in class.
3. Experience before recognition: Students should engage in experiencing music in some way before requiring them to recognize different aspects of the music. Engage them in the musical experience before you discuss it or try to define it in some way.
4. Variety is important: Introduce students to music in a variety of modes, meters, genres, cultural backgrounds, and forms. A wider variety of repertoire will help to support a broader musical vocabulary for students' analysis and evaluation of music in the future.
5. Multiple methods of engagement: Music should be experienced aurally through listening and performing, kinesthetically through movement to music and performing, and visually through iconic representation of music. Experiencing music in more than one way will help to reinforce the musical concepts students are learning.

Rote Song Teaching

One of the basic ways of integrating music into the classroom is by teaching songs to your students. While there are many song-teaching strategies, the rote teaching method outlined below is a clear and direct way to teach students simple songs in class.

1. Introduce the song. What is the title? Is there background information students need to know? How does this song tie in to their learning?
2. Ask a guided listening question to focus students' attention. For example, in the song "This Old Man," you could ask, "Where does this old man play knick-knack?"
3. Perform the song for the students as they listen for the answer to your question. It may help to encourage students to follow the beat of the song by patting or clapping along.
4. Get the answer to your guided listening question to assess how well students were listening to the song.
5. Teach short phrases of the song. Gesture in some clear way for students to echo you. Pointing works well. If the song uses hand gestures, these can also be used to prompt students to echo. A short phrase is usually 4 beats long (strong beats are underlined). For example:
    a. This old man, he played one
    b. He played knick-knack on my thumb
    c. With a knick-knack paddy-whack, give a dog a bone
    d. This old man came rolling home
6. Teach long phrases of the song. Again, gesture for students to echo you. A long phrase usually is the combination of two short phrases. For example:
    a. This old man, he played one. He played knick-knack on my thumb.
    b. With a knick-knack paddy-whack, give a dog a bone. This old man came rolling home.

7. Provide students with a prompt or "ready-sing" to perform the song on their own. This can be sung on the first few pitches of the song, or chanted in tempo if you are teaching a chant or rhyme. (e.g., "1, 2, ready sing"). You should not sing with the students as they perform so that you can accurately assess their musicianship. You may prompt with hand gestures and occasionally mouth words if necessary. Don't be concerned if the performance is not perfect. This gives you an opportunity to hear what parts of the song they need to review.

8. Provide positive but honest feedback to the students about their performance. What did they do well? Where do they need to improve?

Keep in mind that shorter songs or single verses will be more appropriate for younger students to learn via the rote song teaching method. Older students will be able to learn longer songs by rote.

Integration of Music into Curricular Areas

Integrating music into lessons may be accomplished in two ways. The most common method used by elementary teachers is to find a song or musical recording on a specific topic to use as a complement to a lesson in a specific area. This approach tends to prioritize non-musical curricular goals over actual curricular integration. An alternate approach involves identifying complementary skill sets within music and the content area you are teaching so that the lesson will have a more balanced approach toward accomplishing both musical and non-musical goals. Regardless of which approach you take to curricular integration of music, careful planning of your lessons will help you identify both musical and non-musical objectives as well as strategies to assess student learning. The following section on lesson planning will provide general guidelines for lesson planning that can be adopted in any curricular area. A clear approach to planning is essential regardless of the content you are teaching and will provide a solid foundation for your instruction.

Lesson Planning

Writing an effective lesson plan begins with a solid objective and an assessment that clearly demonstrates the student's success at achieving that objective.

Teaching Concept and Grade Level: Knowing the appropriate age for specific concepts takes time and experience. If you're unsure, ask someone who teaches your target grade level, or try some of these places:

- State or national standards on the appropriate websites.
- Many school systems have written benchmarks for various grade levels.
- Teacher editions for classroom texts: check the table of contents.

Objectives: You need to have an objective that clearly identifies the concept or skill that you are addressing your lesson. BE SPECIFIC about what it is you want them to know. Keep asking yourself "What do I want students to know about this?"

If you have a broad concept, such as "The Civil War" or "Parts of Speech," you will need to narrow it down to "The Battle of Gettysburg" or "Adjectives."

Once you have identified the concept, you need to consider the exact skill or knowledge bits that you will address in your lesson. What is it about the Battle of Gettysburg that you want the class to learn in this lesson? Do you want them to know the events leading to it? The participants and the leadership strategies? The death tolls and subsequent repercussions?

Limit yourself to one or two behavioral objectives. This is usually recommended for lower elementary classrooms. Trying to teach too many objectives at one time causes confusion, and less learning. A broad concept such as colors would be broken down into several separate lessons, including identification of colors, order of colors in the rainbow, mixing primary colors to create secondary colors, and similar subject areas.

Name: _____

PRACTICE

For each broad concept below, name at least three narrower concepts.

1. Kindergarten science: the seasons

2. Third-grade social studies: state and local industries

3. Fourth-grade language arts: writing a letter

4. Second-grade math:

5. Fifth-grade social studies: American Westward Movement

Stating Your Objective: Your objective statement contains two parts: It states the specific information or skill students will have as a result of your lesson, and it names the assessment tool. It usually appears in a form something like this:

- TLW (The Learner Will) demonstrate understanding of _____ by _____.

Replace the words "understanding of" by a more appropriate verb if necessary, such as "ability to" or "recognition of."

Your objective should have an action word in it, after the word "by." What action will the students have to perform that will demonstrate their new knowledge? Will they sort, act out, or perform? Avoid sedentary verbs, such as "recite" or "list," which simply ask students to regurgitate material. Consider action verbs such as: composing, interpreting, performing, moving, analyzing, improvising, describing, critiquing, synthesizing, and categorizing. This part of the objective should match the type of assessment that you will use to determine understanding. If your lesson is integrating musical material to supplement student learning, be sure to include this as part of your objective.

Examples:

- TLW demonstrate understanding of the water cycle by correctly labeling the processes of evaporation, condensation, and precipitation on a chart.
- *Integrating music*—TLW demonstrate understanding of the water cycle by composing and performing a song that correctly expresses the processes of evaporation, condensation, and precipitation.
- TLW demonstrate the ability to correctly use adjectives by writing a descriptive paragraph in which at least ten adjectives are used and underlined.
- *Integrating music*—TLW demonstrate understanding of adjectives by circling all of the adjectives in the lyrics of a song used in class and identifying appropriate classroom percussion sounds to represent the adjectives.

Assessment: Now that you have named your assessment tool in the objective statement, you need to specify clearly what this assessment will look like. If you are using a written assessment, such as a true/false, multiple choice, or fill in the blank, specify how many questions will you have and what percentage will denote success.

Be sure that the actions in your assessment are appropriate for the objective. For example, if you want students to demonstrate a skill, then your assessment must include a situation that asks the student to perform that task, not just describe it or categorize it. For example, if your objective is for students to be able to be able to read aloud using correct vowel sounds, you would need to provide an opportunity for students to do that.

It is necessary to use an assessment tool that is age appropriate (limit paper-and-pencil tests for kindergarten or first-grade to matching, identification, drawing, or other grade-appropriate activities) and manageable (consider your time and resources—do you really have the time to listen to each child count aloud by 5s to 100?). Set up your rubric so that you can assess each student individually or as part of a smaller group. Be specific about the criteria used in grading.

For essays or presentation projects (dioramas, essays, posters, book reports), what specific things will you look for? In this case a rubric would be appropriate. A typical elementary rubric for writing a paragraph might look something like this:

- 3 points: Student has written at least three sentences with a main idea and two supporting sentences, uses correct punctuation and grammar.
- 2 points: Student has written fewer than three sentences, has a main idea and one supporting sentences, or has the correct number of sentences and has punctuation and/or grammar errors.

- 1 point: Student has written fewer than three sentences, with a main idea and weak support. May contain punctuation and/or grammar errors.

Although teacher observation is a valid form of assessment, you will need to have a quantitative measurement for purposes of recording achievement. How often does the child need to demonstrate the correct skill or behavior in order to show success? You would need to make a statement such as: "The student will demonstrate success by giving the correct letter sound on four out of five attempts."

If your objective integrates music as part of student learning, you will need to consider how you will assess musical performance or student musical listening. You can use simple rubrics to assess intonation, rhythm, use of singing voice, and adherence to lyrics in musical performance. To assess musical listening, you can create a visual listening guide for students to follow, or you can ask students to give a visual indicator such as a specific movement when they hear a change in the music.

Name: _____

PRACTICE

Name an appropriate assessment tool for each objective. For one of the objectives, indicate how music might be used to demonstrate learning.

1. (Fifth grade) Students will demonstrate understanding of the major causes of the Revolutionary War by:

2. (Third grade) Students will demonstrate knowledge of the three layers of the rainforest by:

3. (Kindergarten) Students will demonstrate knowledge of the three primary colors by:

4. (Second grade) Students will demonstrate understanding of the process of subtraction with regrouping by:

Lesson Plan Format

LESSON PLAN TOPIC: **TITLE:**

AUTHOR (you):

GRADE: **Integrated Disciplines:**

State or National Benchmarks:

OBJECTIVE:

ASSESSMENT:

MATERIALS:

List everything you need to have in order to teach your lesson. This includes handouts, writing utensils, recordings, CD player, posters, etc. If using a book, give a full citation.

PROCEDURES:

Anticipatory Set: Access prior knowledge. Don't begin by asking if students know anything about your concept (if they already knew, why would you need to teach it?). Begin with something related, that they are already familiar with.

Vocabulary: What words will students need to understand in order to participate in your lesson? Anything that's not part of the everyday vocabulary of the students you are teaching should be reviewed.

Instruction: This can include lecture, a video, a piece of literature, or discussion.

Guided Practice Activities: (address at least two different learning styles—at least one should require students to get out of their seats, especially at lower elementary grades)

1. First guided practice   **2.** Second guided practice

CLOSURE:

Sample Lesson Plan

LESSON PLAN TOPIC Cause and Effect   **TITLE:** What if?

AUTHOR: Patricia Gordon

GRADE: 2   **Integrated Discipline(s):** Music and Language Arts

Michigan STANDARDS: English Language Arts/Strand VI/Content Standard 8/Early Elementary, Benchmark 3:

Explore how the characteristics of various informational genres (e.g., show-and-tell, trade books, textbooks, and dictionaries) and elements of expository text structure (e.g., organizational patterns, major ideas, and details) can be used to convey ideas.

OBJECTIVE: TLW demonstrate understanding of cause/effect by drawing a cartoon strip depicting a chain of events precipitated by a single event.

TLW demonstrate understanding of speech rhythms by correctly performing a recurring refrain in the story and maintaining the beat by clapping or using body percussion.

MATERIALS:

- Book, *Bringing the Rain to Kapiti Plain*, by Verna Aardema. Published by Dial Books, New York, 1981.

- cash register tape

- pencils, crayons or colored pencils

- small sheets w/sample "causes"

PROCEDURES:

Anticipatory Set (access prior learning)

Discussion begun by teacher: "What would happen if you dripped chocolate ice cream all over your best clothes?" Accept possible answers—one might involve mom! Then, "If your mom came to wipe the ice cream off you and she slipped and fell in the ice cream, what might happen?" "What would happen if she slid into the dog, who was sleeping?" etc.

Instruction

When one thing makes something else happen, this is called "cause and effect." Listen to the story about a boy who lives in Africa. He sees that his animals are starving because there is no rain and the grass is brown and dead, so he has to do something about it. He does something that makes something else happen, and that makes something else happen, and so on.

Read the story, encouraging students to join in at the end of each segment on "The big, black cloud, all heavy with rain, That shadowed the ground on Kapiti Plain." [Musical integration] Demonstrate that the words have a strong beat and rhythm by keeping the beat (clapping or other body percussion).

Activities for Guided Practice

1. After reading the story, discuss with the class what Ki-pat did to help the animals. What happened first? What happened next?
2. Select three volunteers to come to the front of the room and have them line up side by side. Ask, "If I smile and do something nice to (the first person), what might he do when he sees (the second person)? And what will happen when he or she sees (the third person)? So since I was nice to (first), he was nice to (second), and she was nice to (third). The first nice thing made the second nice thing happen, and the second nice thing made the third thing happen."
3. Have class split into pairs. Give each pair a situation where one person causes something to happen, and give the students time to decide what the effect would be. If there is time, let them try to figure out a secondary effect. After five minutes of planning, each group should share its situation, explaining the cause and the effect.

Independent Practice

Give each child a length of wide cash register tape or a construction paper strip about 6" by 18" with three rectangles drawn on it, like cartoon frames. In the first frame, students should draw an event chosen from a list of suggestions given by the teacher (a bad storm, food left out at a campsite, etc.). In the second frame, students should draw or describe an effect of that situation. The third frame should be used for a secondary effect.

ASSESSMENT: Students will be assessed on their cartoons according to the following rubric:

0 - no cartoon
1 - unidentifiable cause and effect
2 - either cause or effect is unidentifiable
3 - identifiable cause and effect

CLOSURE:

Cartoon strips will be displayed in the room and shared with the class.

Name: _____

PRACTICE

For one of the following curricular areas, choose a lesson topic and write a sample plan using the format presented in this chapter. Your plan should integrate musical engagement within the procedures.

Music and Math
- Pattern recognition and spatial awareness
- Notation algebra
- Duration of time

Music and Science
- Acoustics
- Scientific method and discovery
- Environmental sounds

Music and Language Arts
- Storytelling
- Syllables, accents, and speech patterns
- Creative writing and composition

Music and Social Studies
- World culture
- Historical culture
- Societal issues

LESSON PLAN TOPIC: TITLE:

AUTHOR:

GRADE: Integrated Disciplines:

State or National Benchmarks:

OBJECTIVE:

ASSESSMENT:

MATERIALS:

PROCEDURES:

Anticipatory Set:

Vocabulary:

Instruction:

Guided Practice Activities: (address at least two different learning styles—at least one should require students to get out of their seats, especially at lower elementary grades)

    1. First guided practice

    2. Second guided practice

CLOSURE:

MUSICAL RESOURCES AND REFERENCES
Song Examples and Alterations for the Classroom

This Old Man

Traditional English Nursery Rhyme

This song can also be chanted on text, used as a rhythm round, or played on body percussion: quarter note = stomp, eighth note = clap, sixteenth note = pat

Charlie Over the Ocean

In the original game, one child is selected to walk around the outside of the circle singing the *call* phrases as the rest of the class sings the *response*. On "Can't catch me," the child on the outside taps someone on the shoulder to chase him or her around the circle. I recommend altering this for safety reasons. The last phrase can be changed to "Could've been me," and the child tapped on the shoulder will join the original student marching around the outside and become the new leader of the *call* and *response* in the song. Eventually, all children will join the outside line or circle marching around.

My Bonnie

Traditional Scottish Folk Song

In this singing game, children are challenged to stand up and/or sit down on each word beginning with the letter B. As an alternative, you can have some students begin standing and others begin sitting. If the standing and sitting becomes too cumbersome, you can have students clap or create another motion on the words beginning with B.

This song works well for beginning folk dances with its ABA form.

Shoo Fly

- Simple version:
  - o "Shoo fly" section: Children walk into the circle for four steps, out for four steps, REPEAT.
  - o "I feel like a morning star" section: Children walk clockwise eight steps, then counter-clockwise eight steps.
  - o "Shoo fly" section repeats.

- Advanced version:
  - o "Shoo fly" section: Children walk into the circle for four steps, out for four steps, REPEAT.
  - o "I feel like a morning star" section: Holding hands in the circle, one student leader will walk towards and underneath the bridge created by two adjoined hands of students on the opposite side of the circle. As all hands are connected, this will invert the circle. (Lyrics may need to repeat until circle is inverted)
  - o "Shoo fly" section: Same as in first step, but children are facing out of the circle.
  - o Optional: Reverse the circle by having the student leader back up through the bridged hands on "I feel" section until circle returns to original formation.

Recommended Song Collections

- *Get America Singing Again, volumes 1, 2* (Hal Leonard, 1996)
- *Roots and Branches,* compiled by Patricia Shehan Campbell, Ellen McCullough-Brabson, Judith Cook Tucker (World Music Press, 1994)
- *My Little Rooster (vol. 1), Bought Me a Cat (vol. 2), John the Rabbit (vol. 3), The Little Black Bull (vol. 4)—Folk Songs, Singing Games, and Play Parties for Kids of All Ages* compiled by Jill Trinka (GIA Publications, 2006)

Recommended Online Resources

- Smithsonian Folkways: www.folkways.si.edu
- The American Folksong Collection: http://kodaly.hnu.edu
- Songs for Teaching: http://songsforteaching.com/index.html
- Bus Songs, Children's Songs and Nursery Rhymes: http://bussongs.com
- Mama Lisa's World, International Songs: www.mamalisa.com/index.html
- KiDiddles Children's Music: www.kididdles.com
- Mathwire Math Music: www.mathwire.com/music/music.html

Sample Lesson Plans

LESSON PLAN TOPIC: Measuring and fractions   **TITLE:** Measuring for Music

GRADE: 2   **Integrated Disciplines:** Music and Math

Michigan STANDARDS: Math: Strand I (Numbers and Operations)/Strand III (Measurement)

OBJECTIVES:

TLW demonstrate an understanding of simple fractions by correctly measuring and marking a piece of yarn for 1/2, 1/3, 1/4, 1/6

TLW demonstrate an understanding of the relationship between length and pitch by performing simple melodies on a single piece of yarn.

ASSESSMENT:

1. Yarn will be placed in envelopes or folders marked with students' names and the measurements taken in class. Measurements will be assessed for accuracy.
2. Each pair of students will perform their familiar string melody for the teacher, singing along to indicate accuracy of pitch.

MATERIALS:

Rulers, markers, yarn, envelopes, guitar (or other string instrument), wooden dowels of varying lengths to represent different fractions (whole, half, third, fourth, sixth)

PROCEDURES:

Anticipatory Set:

1. 5 student volunteers at the front of the classroom each hold up a wooden dowel. Students in the class estimate which dowel represents 1/2, 1/3, 1/4, and 1/6

Instruction:

1. After all students are seated, teacher demonstrates the sound of an open string plucked on a guitar.
2. Ask: "If I divide the string in half, will the sound be higher or lower?"
3. Demonstrate changes in pitch by fretting the string in different spots.

Activity for Guided Practice:

1. Each student receives a long piece of yarn in an envelope, a ruler, and a marker
2. Using the rulers, have students measure the length of his or her string (most pieces should be about 24 inches long). Students write their names and the length of the measurements on the outside of the envelope in which they receive their strings.
3. Folding the string in half, students measure and mark the 1/2 length. Compare numbers (should be around 12 inches).
4. Repeat step 3, folding the string in thirds, fourths, and sixths.

Independent Practice:

1. Place students in pairs. One student holds an end of the string to his or her ear while the partner holds the other end taut. The student 'listening' plucks the string to hear the vibration.
2. The partner, still pulling the string taut, pinches the string at the 1/2 mark. The listener plucks the string to hear the resulting higher pitch.

3. The partners repeat step 2 at the 1/3, 1/4, and 1/6 marks.
4. Partners switch roles and repeat the procedure again.
5. Using trial and error, the partners cooperate to recreate simple melodies such as "Mary Had a Little Lamb" or "Hot Cross Buns" on their strings.

CLOSURE:
Teacher will use the guitar to perform the simple melodies found by students for the whole class. Students may sing along.

LESSON PLAN TOPIC: Parts of Speech   **TITLE:** Musical Mad-libs

GRADE: 4   **Integrated Disciplines:** Music and Language Arts

Michigan Standards: English Language Arts: Strand I (Reading, Word Recognition)/Strand II (Writing, Grammar and Usage)

OBJECTIVE:

TLW demonstrate and understanding of nouns, adjectives, verbs, and adverbs by correctly identifying these parts of speech within lyrics of a song and by replacing them with new words.

ASSESSMENT:

Musical Mad-lib will be assessed using the following checklist for a total of 6 points:

___ Song performed with appropriate singing voice
___ Song includes at least 6 replacements words
___ Song includes new nouns
___ Song includes new adjectives
___ Song includes new adverbs
___ Song includes new verbs

MATERIALS: Lyrics to familiar simple songs (Row, Row; Mary Had a Little Lamb; This Old Man; I'm a Little Teapot; London Bridge, etc.); short spider story, projector, pencils and paper.

PROCEDURES:

Vocabulary: Noun, Adjective, Verb, Adverb

Anticipatory Set:

1. Display on the projector and read the following short story to students:
   There once was a family of tiny brown spiders who lived in a big green garden. They spent their days spinning silk into big sticky webs. To build their webs, they had to run, jump, swing, and weave in many different directions with their silk. In the evening, they would creep to different parts of their webs and remain still, waiting for big, juicy bugs to fly into the sticky strands of silk. The youngest spider was very fast. As soon as a bug was caught in the web, he would quickly jump upon it and make it his dinner. The oldest spider was not as quick, but she was very stealthy. When a bug landed in her web, she would slowly creep toward her dinner, and surprise it from behind.
2. Ask students the following questions:
   a. Who lived in the garden? What did they build? (nouns)
   b. What type of spiders were they? How would you describe their webs? (adjectives)
   c. What did the spiders do to build their webs? (verbs)
   d. How did the youngest spider jump upon his dinner? How did the oldest spider creep toward her dinner? (adverbs)

Instruction:

1. As a class, have students identify all of the nouns in the story. On the projector (or SmartBoard), highlight nouns in green
   a. Identify and highlight adjectives in yellow
   b. Identify and highlight verbs in purple
   c. Identify and highlight adverbs in blue
2. Display on projector a version of the story with select nouns, adjectives, verbs, and adverbs removed. Leave a highlighted blank in those spots to be filled in.
   a. Have students suggest alternate words to fill in the blanks of the story.

3. Remove the display of the story.
   a. Ask students for suggestion for random nouns, adjectives, verbs, and adverbs.
   b. Use the random new words in the blanks and read the story again—this version will be much sillier.

Independent Practice:

1. Hand out copies of lyrics to familiar songs (Row, Row; Mary Had a Little Lamb; This Old Man; I'm a Little Teapot; London Bridge, etc.).
   a. Sing through the songs as a class
2. Each student chooses a song from the list to turn into a musical Mad-lib.
   a. Students individually circle and label the parts of speech they can replace.
3. In pairs or small groups, students ask each other for new words without revealing the original songs they have chosen.
4. Students use the new words suggested by peers to create new silly versions of the songs.

CLOSURE:

Students take turns performing the new musical Mad-libs for the class.

LESSON PLAN TOPIC: American Revolutionary War   **TITLE:** The Musical Voice of the People

GRADE: 5   **Integrated Disciplines:** Music and Social Studies

Michigan Standards: USHG Era 3—Revolution and the New Nation/Causes of the American Revolution; P3.1—Identifying and Analyzing Public Issues

OBJECTIVES:

TLW demonstrate an understanding of American public sentiment during the time before the American Revolution by identifying and describing the context of the issues mentioned in "The Revolutionary Alphabet"

TLW demonstrate an understanding of current public sentiment by composing and performing a new alphabet song, chant, or rap.

ASSESSMENT:

1. In small groups, students will present to their explanations for the facts mentioned within their assigned verse of "The Revolutionary Alphabet," Presentations will be assessed for accuracy of content.

2. Student compositions will be assessed for originality, clarity of performance, and accuracy of content.

MATERIALS

Recording and lyrics to "The Revolutionary Alphabet" (available at Smithsonian Folkways: www .folkways.si.edu/TrackDetails.aspx?itemid=7179Internet access/computer lab

PROCEDURES:

Anticipatory Set:

1. Ask students to name songs they are familiar with that cover topics such as war, protest, and peace. These may be folk songs or popular songs.
2. Discuss how the songwriters conveyed their messages in the songs. Were there any (school appropriate) lyrics that stood out and resonated with the listener?

Instruction:

1. Hand out copies of lyrics to "The Revolutionary Alphabet."
   a. As the recording plays, direct students to circle the lines that contain facts they are familiar with.
   b. Play recording.
2. Teach the chorus: "Stand firmly A to Z, We swear forever to be free!"
   a. Play recording a second time; students sing the chorus each time it enters.

Guided Practice:

1. Split students into 6 groups (one group for each verse of the song).
   a. In groups, students will share the items they've circled as containing familiar facts.
   b. For each letter of the alphabet containing an unknown reference, the group must search for the context or explanation online.

2. Each group will compose its modern version of the alphabet song. This may be sung to the tune of "The Revolutionary Alphabet," another familiar melody, or it may be chanted or rapped.

    a. The new versions of the alphabets should contain facts relevant to present day issues and concerns (locally, statewide, nationally, and/or globally).

CLOSURE:

1. Each group will present findings on its verse of "The Revolutionary Alphabet"
2. Each group will perform its modern version of the alphabet song.

LESSON PLAN TOPIC: Animal Habitats   **TITLE:** Living Soundscapes

GRADE: 5   **Integrated Disciplines:** Music and Science

Michigan Standards: Life Science—Evolution/Environmental Adaptation

OBJECTIVES:

TLW demonstrate an understanding of environmental adaptation by describing, drawing, and labeling imaginary animals designed to function well in specific habitats (grassland, rainforest, swamp, deciduous forest)

TLW demonstrate an understanding of how life functions within a habitat by creating and performing soundscapes to represent environmental sounds.

ASSESSMENT:

1. Animal designs will be assessed for originality and appropriateness of adaptations to a given environment.
2. Soundscapes will be recorded at the end of the lesson. One week later, the soundscapes will be played back to the class. Students will use aural clues to decide which habitat each soundscape represents.

MATERIALS

Habitat chart, paper, colored pencils, classroom instruments/body percussion/found objects for soundscapes, digital audio recorder

PROCEDURES:

Vocabulary: habitat, grassland, rainforest, swamp, deciduous forest, soundscape

Anticipatory Set:

1. Discuss with class the different characteristics of the following habitats: grassland, rainforest, freshwater marsh, and deciduous forest
2. On the board have students list animals that reside in the different habitats

Instruction:

1. For each habitat and animal listed on the board, discuss what characteristics of the animal allow it to thrive in that environment.
2. Consider the following for each animal:
   a. Life cycle
   b. Predators and prey
   c. Physical adaptations
   d. Sounds and communication
   e. Relationship between animals and plant life in the habitats

Guided Practice:

1. Divide the class into four groups (one for each habitat).
2. Using body percussion, classroom instruments, and found objects, each group will compose a soundscape illustrating the audible environment of the habitat.
3. After students are given time to create and practice, each group will perform its soundscape for the class. Soundscapes are to be digitally recorded.

Independent Practice:

1. Each student will be assigned one of the four habitats. Independently, each student must create an imaginary animal with physical adaptations designed to thrive in the assigned habitat.
2. Students will draw a diagram of the new animal, labeling the different structures on the animal's body and listing the adaptive characteristics.

CLOSURE:

1. Animal diagrams will be displayed in the room, grouped by habitat.
2. Soundscape recordings will be played back a week later for students to recall the corresponding habitats illustrated by the compositions.

WORKS CITED

Elliot, David. *Music Matters: A New Philosophy of Music Education* (New York: Oxford University Press, 1995), 124.

Gordon, Edwin, E. *Preparatory Audiation, Audiation, and Music Learning Theory: A Handbook of a Comprehensive Music Learning Sequence* (Chicago: GIA Publications, Inc., 2001), 3.

Jensen, Eric. *Art with the Brain in Mind* (Alexandria, VA: ASCD, 2001), 14.

National Coalition for Core Arts Standards, "National Core Arts Standards", http://www.nationalartsstandards.org/

Reimer, Bennett. *A Philosophy of Music Education: Advancing the Vision* (Upper Saddle River: Pearson Education, 2003), 11.

Rutkowski, Joanne, and Runfola, Maria. *TIPS: The Child Voice* (Reston, VA: MENC, 1997), 3-4.

Small, Christopher. *Musicking: The Meanings of Performers and Listening* (Middletown: Wesleyan University Press, 1998), 2-3.

Wade, Bonnie. *Thinking Musically: Experiencing Music, Expressing Culture* (New York: Oxford University Press, 2004), 1-2.

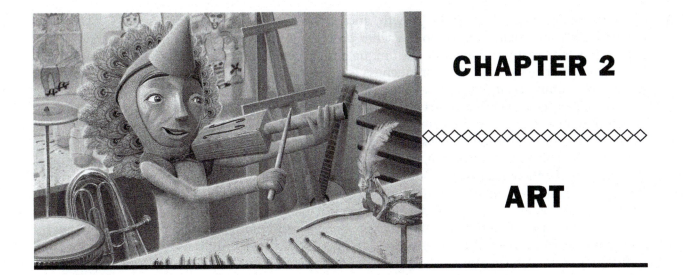

CHAPTER 2

⋈⋈⋈⋈⋈⋈⋈⋈⋈⋈⋈⋈⋈⋈⋈

ART

THEORY OF ART EDUCATION AND TEACHING PHILOSOPHY

This chapter discusses historical developments and current issues in art education the philosophy and theories that drive these reforms, and their effect on the role of teachers and on curriculum changes and visual arts learning in schools. Each movement shapes curriculum structures, redefining what art is thought to be and how it is valued. It also dictates what genres of art should be taught and learned based on various scopes of meaning, depending upon whose interests are under consideration and upon the interplay of ideologies as they relate to the historical context.

> A work of art is . . . a representation of the world outside of art—often the everyday social world. . . . Within general education, the purpose of art education is *not* to induct individuals into the world of the professional fine arts community . . . [it] is to enable individuals to find meaning in the world of art for life in the everyday world.[1]

The Artistic and Creativity Movement of the 1960s: Stages of Artistic Development

Historically, the value of art has resided in its aesthetic quality, with instruction often emphasizing artistic and aesthetic experiences related to individual expression and creativity.[2] Views of what is relevant in the art classroom have often shifted depending on the current movements and teaching philosophies. These phenomena have similarly affected views of the importance of art education at the elementary level. Lowenfeld's[3] psychological studies concerning children's art established a rubric for children's development in art, and the theory articulated in his book *Creative and Mental Growth* facilitated an understanding of the stages of childhood developmental growth as expressed in art, in the process becoming one of the most influential textbooks in art education. Lowenfeld's

---

[1] Arthur Efland, *Art and Cognition: Integrting the Visual Arts in the Curriculum* (New York: Teachers College: Columbia University, 2002), 121.

[2] ———, "Antecedents of Discipline-Based Art Education," *Journal of Aesthetic Education* 21, no. 2, Special Issue: Discipline-Based ArtEducation (1987).

[3] Viktor Lowenfeld, *Viktor Lowenfeld Speaks on Art and Creativity* ([Washington,: National Art Education Association, 1968); Viktor Lowenfeld and W. Lambert Brittain, *Creative and Mental Growth*, 4th ed. (New York,: Macmillan, 1964).

methodology to assess the child's growth, and of the characteristics of children's art, has often been adapted into elementary school teacher preparation programs. For Lowenfeld,[4] individual expression and creativity constitute the unique domain of art, and such experience constitutes the major goal of art education. This uniqueness is what drives art as a separate subject from others in the curriculum because it represents the single contribution of the arts that other subjects can't supply—the artistic experience. Art education should provide children with the conditions under which they may express and create, and it should expose children to the exploration of various materials and media for self expression. Such aesthetic experiences can assist children's aesthetic/ artistic, social, physical/perceptual, intellectual/linguistic, and emotional/moral development.[5]

Lowenfeld's theory concerning the stages of children's artistic development provides a methodology to evaluate a child's art, not only through a better understanding of a child's physical, social, emotional, and intellectual development, but also by the child's progress through certain stages of development in their artistic creation. Such a curriculum cultivates individual creativity and emphasizes individual progress. Art activities should help children develop skills through individual exploration of the creative process and focus on the aesthetic quality of materials—how things feel, look, smell, taste, and sound—and what these things, once the necessary skills are acquired, can do when combined via the operation of one's senses assembled according to a personal schema in the stages of development. (see Figure 2.1 for Lowenfeld's six stages of children's development in art).

[4] Lowenfeld and Brittain, *Creative and Mental Growth.*
[5] Carolyn Boriss-Krimsky, "Stages of Artistic Development," in *The Creativity Handbook: A Visual Arts Guide for Parents and Teachers* (Springfield: Charles C Thomas Publisher, 1999).

Figure 2.1. Lowenfeld's (1964) six stages of children's development in art.[6]

Lowenfeld's stages	1. Scribbling and mark making	2. Pre-schematic and early symbol making	3. Schematic and symbol making
Child's drawing			
Ages	2–4	4–7	7–9
Grades	Pre-school	Kindergarden	1–3
Characteristics	Marking making: Children at this stage already evince emotional development, giving thoughts and feelings to inanimate objects and challenging their perception and memory. Their motor skills are more mature, and they are able to draw lines and angles. The coordination of hand and eye movements are increasingly challenged, enhancing skills in formal rendering of recognizable objects. Drawings tend to evince demands made on controlling markings. Children sometimes name objects based on their preferences. Alex, a 2-year-old boy, here draws controlled circles and lines, calling the circular objects "eyes" and the rectangular boxes "teeth."	Representational attempts: Children at this stage are egocentric; everything they draw concerns what they know well around them. A 4-year-old, Queenie, draws herself with long hair, wearing a skirt. She draws things that fit her own schema (using symbols to represent what she knows). At this stage, children tend to draw humans in a sort of tadpole form, with head and body rendered as circles, and arms and legs protruding from the body. The children have little understanding of space and proportion, and evince little concern with using the colors of reality. In the above drawing, for instance, the apple is larger than the head.	Forming a concept of reality: In the symbol making stage, children's thinking becomes more reasoned, logical, and organized, and they begin to think in terms of concrete and tangible information. This drawing by a 7-year-old girl, Melody, illustrates many symbols organized around the spaces of her life; she draws what she sees from images of popular media (from TV, movies, school books, and comic books), and things which emerge from her life, such as a fountain, flowers, a tree, a rabbit, a girl, a cat, and a pig, and a house. In the sky she draws a sun surrounded by clouds. In this drawing, she has successfully represented people, places, buildings, trees, and structures.

(Continued)

[6] Ibid; Lowenfeld and Brittain, *Creative and Mental Growth*.

60

Figure 2.1. (Continued)

Lowenfeld's Stages	4. Realism in drawing and emerging expertise	5. Pseudo-realism and artistic challenges	6. Period of decision and artistic thinking
Ages	9–11	11–13	14–17
Grades	3–5	5–7 (middle school)	8–11 (high school)
Characteristics	At this stage, children become aware of the process of drawing realistically and become extremely critical about self presentation—how things look or appear to them. They will erase an object until they make it right, not in a realistic sense, but in line with an experience they have of it. They start to pay attention to and develop an awareness of space between the baseline and the skyline. Hank, a 9-year-old boy, no longer draws objects standing on a base line; he uses overlapping of objects to represent spatial relationships. His rendering of a jeep and a man standing between two mountains makes evident the use of small and large objects to create three-dimensional effects regarding spatial relationships, in a way defined not by objective sense, but by feelings but by objective sense, to portray his experiences with objects as they appear in his environment.	At this stage, children have the ability to draw more accurately and with more detail, and they strive for a more personal style. The final production is more important than the process. They have obtained skills related to light, shade, and perspective, and they can create texture and depth. They often draw upon memory, emphasizing subjective interpretations of emotional and social contexts—how the world relates to them. Allen, a 13-year-old middle school student, has painted a landscape related to a trip with his father, using warm colors and detailed color changes across various textures, reflecting his emotional and nostalgic reaction to the family trip.	This stage reflects the adolescent's need for investigating the self before entering adulthood. Lisa, 17, an art student, creates a portrait of Allen, which exhibits conscious decision making through exploring with media, styles, and techniques. She is critically aware of her drawing skill on the representation of realism as well as on the finished product itself.

The concept of "left alone, children draw representationally when they are ready" is often reflected in the art curriculum because many teachers are afraid to destroy children's natural creative impulses by instructing what they can draw or imposing ideas upon them. Art activities based on Lowenfeld's creative learning model, often emphasize building children's observational, perceptual, and realistic drawing skills.

As children progress toward adulthood, it is believed, their capacity for artistic expression begins to fade. Pedagogically, we should strive to maintain this innate ability (based on Lowenfeld's stages of artistic development[7]) as much as possible in the elementary school setting. Despite the personal aesthetic biases of, the art curriculum and related activities should emphasize the learner's cognitive development in relation to social and cultural contexts rather than from a subjective position. Duncum[8] discusses a variety of approaches to integrating art into the elementary classroom so as to help teachers evaluate children's work and help them develop an understanding of their own work and skills using verbal reflection including conversational, perceptual, conventional, non-sequenced, and inductive strategies. These strategies help pre-service teachers evaluate and respond to children's artwork (see Figure 2.2 for Duncum's strategies for integrating art into the elementary classroom).

Figure 2.2.   Duncum's (1999) strategies for integrating art into the elementary classroom.

Duncum's Strategy	Concept Defined	Methods of Integrating Art into the Elementary Classroom
Verbal Reflection	Children learn from dialogues between the teacher and themselves. Teachers provide verbal feedback, commenting on the work by asking questions that get the children to think about meanings and to reflect on how they created a piece.	When praised, children benefit from verbal feedback in a specific context. Instead of vague comments—"I like it," or "it is beautiful"—comments should describe the work in detail to assist children with their thinking and meaning-making concerning what they have accomplished, using such formal terms as "tone," "shape," and "balance," and such descriptive terms as "bumpy," "wiggly" and "bright." Students learn to reflect from comments such as "you made a big shape on your paper. Did you use a lot of colors to make the shape?"
Conversational	Children learn from interactions with one another. Teachers provide opportunities for conversation by arranging the classroom so children can work together to create art and learn from each other as they make pictures, whether during daily conversations or by "copying" from their peers. In this case, copying is an excellent technique for helping children learn how to draw based on their peers' artistic sense.	Copying can be a method of learning step-by-step how things are done. "Copying" can take place via the "plus one phenomena" of learning by steps from peers' comments or ideas. Children are motivated to learn from their peers, who represent a model that is only one step ahead of their own.
Perceptual	Children learn from their perceptions of what they see while drawing, paying attention to aspects of the subject, drawing from perceptional experiences of what they see both before and during the process.	Drawing what one sees, not what one knows, the perception process emphasizes the details of the way things are, rather than what one thinks or knows about things.

(Continued)

[7] Lowenfeld and Brittain, *Creative and Mental Growth.*
[8] Paul Duncum, "What Elementary Generalist Teachers Need to Know to Teach Art Well," *Journal of Art Education* 52, no. 6 (1999).

Figure 2.2.   (Continued)

Duncum's Strategy	Concept Defined	Methods of Integrating Art into the Elementary Classroom
Conventional	Children learn from studying other pictures rather than from their lived experiences. Children learn to make images by looking at other images—pre-created pictures. Doing so helps students learn how adults create pictures by recreating them on their own.	Children generally learn best with the aid of visual and auditory information and prompts, visual aids being especially helpful in allowing children to move along in the process of developing their schemas based on the images they consult.
Non-sequence	Children learn to describe others' art by first answering basic questions and later including their own interpretationsof the piece.	Observers ask Who, What, When, Where, and Why about a piece of art. "What is it?" "How was it made?" "Why was it made?"
Inductive	Children learn to draw instances from observations in order to make generalizations.	This strategy is beneficial to upper grades of elementary school children in helping them develop inductive reasoning skills through the process of describing, analyzing, interpreting and finally judging an artwork.

Discipline-Based Art Education (DBAE) of the 1980s: Art as a Subject for Study

The concept of discipline-based art education (DBAE) was developed and implemented in art programs through an effort funded by The Getty Education Institute between the 1980s and 1990s. Through DBAE, the Getty Institute advocated for art's special power to change and educate.[9] This comprehensive approach to art education emerged in response to sociopolitical forces—the need to reexamine art experiences and values. What constitutes art and what counts as knowledge of the arts? What sort of art is worth teaching? Should teachers emphasize style or techniques? Or should art education be judged on how it affects one's emotional and artistic expression? What about cognitive development in arts? Discipline-based art education has encouraged art educators to think about the arts in a different light, to consider the creation of art not only based on the affective domain, but also on whether it brings about excellence in the arts. Smith[10] articulates the rationale behind the DBAE notion of art as a subject for study and as an integral part of education as follows:

> The idea of discipline-based art education acknowledges and builds upon recent developments in the field of art education. It asserts not only that content and procedures for teaching art should be derived from a number of key disciplines but also that the understanding and appreciation of works of art are as educationally valuable as creating art; or that, as one dominant theme of the period in question phrases the new concern, that experiencing works of art aesthetically is as significant as producing them.[11]

Clark, Day, and Greer[12] assert that the visual arts should be an essential part of every child's education, integrating the creation of art and inquiry into the meaning of the arts as primary

[9] Leilani Duke, "The Getty Center for Education in the Arts and Discipline-Based Art Education," *Journal of Art Education* 41, no. 2 (1988); Efland, "Antecedents of Discipline-Based Art Education."

[10] Ralph Smith, "The Changing Image of Art Education: Theoretical Antecedents of Discipline-Based Art Education," *Journal of Aesthetic Education* 21, no. 2, Special Issues: Discipline-Based Art Education (1987).

[11] Ibid.: 4.

[12] Gilbert Clark, Michael Day, and Dwaine Greer, "Discipline-Based Art Education: Becoming Students of Art," *Journal of Aesthetic Education* 21, no. 2, Special Issues: Discipline-Based Art Education (1987).

content, emphasizing how we understand the world and human experiences that transmit cultural values. Instead of teaching individual concepts from each discipline of the arts the curriculum combines experiences from studying four arts disciplines—areas that provide knowledge, skills, and understandings that provide students a broaderview of works of art.[13] DBAE not only teaches studio artmaking, but also integrate art criticism, art history, and aesthetics into the production of art:

(1) Studio Production—making art and learning concepts and skills, including the components of the use of tools, form and structure in the creation of art, expression, and manipulation of materials and media.[14]

(2) Art Criticism—responding to artwork in the examination and discussion of style, and the analysis of formal principals of design, emphasizing elements of art in terms of line, color, shape, composition, and perspective.[15]

(3) Art History—looking at the artwork in its cultural context and at how it may be viewed through social, historical, political, and economic insights, as art history tells us who?, what?, when?, where?, and why?.[16]

(4) Aesthetics—understanding the meaning and value of artwork philosophically—contemplating questions concerning what art is.[17]

These four disciplines together constitute the arts as an important area of study, in the same way other subject areas in school are viewed. Art can be taught and learned through the principle of elements, media driven skills, aesthetic quality, and knowledge of art history in keeping the arts as a separate subject in the curriculum. Not only does art involve aesthetic experience, it also has cognitive value as one contemplates the thinking involved in making art. These four disciplines have come to constitute a primary view of core knowledge in the arts, and pursuing them has come to represent a major goal of art education in the construction of meaning not only in the affective,but in the cognitive domain.[18] As Parsons[19] pointed out, the visual arts require thinking, and this type of thinking can be learned. It is thinking that is as demanding and rewarding as that required for other school subjects that contribute to the development of the developing mind since "artworks are about ideas that derive from social, cultural, and personal worlds and their complex overlapping with materials from other subjects is their educational strength".[20] Thus, art aims to teach for an understanding of one's culture in relation to the world. Curriculum concepts emphasize the importance of teaching art within contexts, art learning through image making, and how visual art is formatted, and how its meaning is formed.[21]

[13] Karen Hamblen, "What Does Dbae Teach?," *Journal of Art Education* 41, no. 2 (1988).

[14] Frederick Spratt, "Art Production in Discipline-Based Art Education," *Journal of Aesthetic Education* 21, no. 2, Special Issues: Discipline-Based Art Edcuation (1987).

[15] Howard Risatti, "Art Criticism in Discipline-Based Art Education," *Journal of Aesthetic Education* 21, no. 2, Special Issue: Discipline-Based Art Education (1987).

[16] Eugene Kleinbauer, "Art History in Discipline-Based Art Education," *Journal of Aesthetic Education* 21, no. 2, Special Issue: Discipline-Based Art Education (1987).

[17] Donald Crawford, "Aesthetics in Discipline-Based Art Educationdonald W. Crawford," *Journal of Aesthetic Education* 21, no. 2, Special Issue: Discipline-Based Art Education (1987).

[18] Efland, "Antecedents of Discipline-Based Art Education.";———, *Art and Cognition: Integrting the Visual Arts in the Curriculum*; Elliot Eisner, *The Arts and Creation of Mind* (New Haven: Yale University Press, 2002).

[19] Michael Parsons, "The Role of the Visual Arts in the Growth of Mind," *Studies in Art Education* 46, no. 4 (2005).

[20] Ibid.: 373.

[21] Efland, *Art and Cognition: Integrting the Visual Arts in the Curriculum*.

Art Education as Visual Cultural Study in the 2000s: The VCAE Approach

The growing interest among art educators and scholars in visual culture has become one of the academic trends of the present day. The art education paradigm has shifted toward a focus on the visual media. This visual movement has been undertaken by many prominent art educators, who include the combination of social and cultural studies in art education as they respond to changes in society.[22] Often, learning in an art classroom is driven by the teacher's desires, interests and values rather than those of the students. As Brent Wilson and Masami Toku[23] observe that motivation plays a central role in the process of making meaning, understanding students' interests outside the classroom motivates students' artmaking and exposes them to means of self-presentation and identification. Such meaning-making will go ahead of the student's understanding of identity. VCAE (Visual Culture Art Education) proponents promote studying images, including those of popular culture, which reflect the students' interests and needs.

This field of study represents a great expansion as it incorporates into the study of art education popular images from nontraditional art forms and cultural sites of everyday experiences, encompassing a wide range of popular artifacts, whether visual, printed, or major media. As Duncum[24] points out, all visual cultural production is available as content, including the traditional fine arts as well as various forms of popular culture (e.g., theme parks, fast food restaurants, computer games, advertisements). Duncum provides the following list as an example:

> Fashion, textiles, pottery and ceramics, hairdryers, shavers, cars, architecture, garden design, advertising, personal, public, corporate and popular images, film, television, computer environments, and games, Internet home pages, newspaper, and magazine design, typography, producers and packing of all kinds.[25]

On the other side of the coin from this opening to popular culture, there is an increasing sense of emergency under which many art educators connect the arts with questions of human existence and issues related to politics, gender, racial and social differences, and by which they challenge unequal power relations and the distribution of the socially dominant values in society.

---

[22] Christine Ballengee-Morris and Patricia Stuhr, "Multicultural Art and Visual Cultural Education in a Changing World," *The Journal of Art Education* 54, no. 4 (2001); Terry Barrett, "Interpreting Visual Culture," *Journal of Art Education* 56, no. 2 (2003); Stephen Carpenter, "An Editorial: The Return of Visual Culture (Why Not?)," *Journal of Art Education* 58, no. 6 (2005); Paul Duncum, "Visual Culture: Developments, Definitions, and Directions for Art Education," *Studies in Art Education* 42, no. 2 (2001);———, "Clarifying Visual Culture Art Education," *The Journal of Art education* 55, no. 3 (2002);———, "Instructional Resources: Visual Culture in the Classroom," *Journal of Art Education* 56, no. 2 (2003); Kerry Freedman, *Teaching Visual Culture: Curriculum, Aesthetics and the Social Life of Art* (New York; Reston, VA: Teachers College Press; National Art Education Association, 2003);———, "The Importance of Student Artistic Production to Teaching Visual Culture," *Journal of Art Education* 56, no. 2 (2003); Karen Keifer-Boyd, Patricia Amburgy, and Wanda Knight, "Three Approches to Teaching Visual Culture in K-12 School Contexts," *Journal of Art Education* 56, no. 2 (2003); Deborah Smith-Shank, "Lewis Hine and His Photo Stories: Visual Culture and Social Reform," *Journal of Art Education* 56, no. 2 (2003); K Tavin, "Hanuntological Shifts: Fear and Loathing of Popular (Visual) Culture," *Studies in Art Education* 46, no. 2 (2005); Pamela Taylor and Christine Ballengee-Morris, "Using Visual Culture to Put a Contemporary "Fizz" On the Study of Pop Art," *Journal of Art Education* 56, no. 2 (2003); Pat Villeneuve, "Why Not Visual Culture?," *Journal of Art Education* 56, no. 2 (2003).

[23] Masami Toku, "What Is Manga?: The Influence of Pop Culture in Adolescent Art," *The Journal of Art Education* 54, no. 2 (2001); Brent Wilson and Masami Toku, "Boys' Love, *Yaoi,* and Art Education: Issues of Power and Pedagogy," in *Semiotics and Art/Visual Culture,* ed. Deborah Smith-Shank (Reston, Virginia: The National Art Education Association, 2003).

[24] Duncum, "Visual Culture: Developments, Definitions, and Directions for Art Education."

[25] Ibid.: 105.

This trend marks the advent of a new role for art educators as cultural agents in making social changes through the visual arts. As Henry Giroux[26] believes strongly, "not only did pedagogy connect questions of form and content, it also introduced a sense of how teaching, learning, textual studies, and knowledge could be addressed as a political issues which foreground considerations of power and social agency," [. . .] and "the demand for linking literature to the life situations of adult learners,"[27] as teachers have insisted that schooling be empowering rather than merely humanizing. The understanding of images and artifacts is no doubt grounded in social and cultural practice. In this paradigm, art becomes a means of critique, comment, and communication concerning issues related to current events. The art curriculum comes to emphasize the lived experience of students (their needs, desires, and interests), rather than being driven by the teacher's desires and interests. It seems that art educators have taken consideration of art in the direction of its contextual creation of meaning in terms of social production and distribution of themes, particularly concerning themselves with the use of artifacts and images in everyday (or popular) cultures, and have taken it away from the museum world, and so-called "high" and "serious" art.

Whether emphasizing art's modernist formal qualities, or pursuing DBAE, a postmodernist thematic approach, or VCAE's contextual inquiry, Sandell[28] proposed that art education should include the three components of the interdisciplinary genre—Form, Theme, and Context—in balancing art education as a field. She characterized this model integrating three aspects of art content as the FTC palette. By exploring the formal qualities of art, students learn about artmaking and the elements of art and the relationship between the design principles. By exploring themes in artwork, students learn about the subject matter, and historical references of art, how these are relevant to other subjects and other art by the integration of themes. By investigating contextual information, students learn to ask when, where, by whom, and why art is made. This contextual investigation also brings a sense of significance and relevance to multiple contexts at the personal, social, cultural, historical, artistic, educational, and political levels. Art education moves from artistic thinking toward a focus on conceptual thinking; the study of big ideas based on issues has thus become an important strategy for designing curricula as part of purposeful planning across the curriculum. The curriculum places an emphasis on inquiry (conceptual framework and key concepts) teaching toward an understanding that uses the big ideas as authentic instruction, thereby empowering students to explore their own meanings and perceive the relevance of the domain to their lives rather than passively accepting meanings from the teacher's direct instruction. The big idea approach will be discussed further in the section entitled Integrated Curriculum.

---

[26] Henry Giroux, *Disturbing Pleasures: Learning Popular Culture* (New York: Routledge, 1994).

[27] Ibid., 131–32.

[28] See Renae Sandell, "Using Form+Theme+Context (Ftc) for Rebalancing 21st-Century Art Education," *Studies in Art Education* 50, no. 3 (2009).

Figure 2.3. The history and philosophy of art education.

	1960s MODERNISM	1980s DBAE	1990s POSTMODERNISM	2000s VCAE
TEACHING PHILOSOPHY	Viktor Lowenfeld's theory concerning creative and mental growth. Self-centered, emphasizing individual progress. Emphasizes art as experience based on feeling rather than knowing.	Michael Day's Discipline Based Art Education (DBAE) Teacher directed. The arts become disciplines and areas of core knowledge.	1990s Elliot Eisner's Postmodern era: art education as cognition. The arts become important subjects in meaning making.	2000s art education as visual cultural study (VCAE). All visual cultural production is available as content.
CURRICULUM DESIGN	The curriculum emphasizes individual exploration of the artmaking process and the quality of materials: how things feel, look, smell, taste, sound, and what they can do.	The curriculum is teacher-driven. The arts become disciplines in the areas of: (1) Studio Production—the components of artmaking, including the use of tools, forms, and means of expression, and manipulating the materials and media. (2) Art Criticism—the examination and discussion of style, analysis of formal principals of design and elements of art in terms of line, color, shape, composition, perspective, and texture. (3) Art History—looking at art in the context of social, historical, political, and economic insights in relating the past to the present. (4) Aesthetics—philosophical questions concerning what art is.	Art should be at the center, at the "core" of the curriculum, connecting subjects with the skills and content interrelated within them. The curriculum encourages students to try making meaning, to read, and to conceptualize a situation.	Curriculum is supported through published research that gives educational validity so as to include students' interests, needs and desires (lived experiences). All visual cultural production is available as content, including the traditional fine arts as well as various forms of popular culture, folk traditions of artmaking, photography, commercial illustration, the various entertainment media including cinema and television, and their electronic extensions via the computer and the Internet (i.e., theme parks, fast food restaurants, computer games, advertisements).

INSTRUCTIONAL STRATEGIES	Subject to personal aesthetic biases. Emphasizes form and structure in the creation of art, stages of artistic development and their effects on one's feelings.	Teacher-driven, the method seeks to teach the fine art culture. Art can be taught and learned through principles of elements, media-driven skills, aesthetic quality, and knowledge of art history.	Emphasizes learning through a thematic approach centered on how visual art is formatted and how it forms meaning. Instructional strategies emphasize methods of motivating students, delivering information, and ensuring that learners are clear about what is expected of them.	Emphasizes learning within multiple contexts. Investigates art as a means of critique, comment and communication with regard to issues related to current events. The curriculum emphasizes inquiry (conceptual framework and key concepts) and teachestoward an understanding using big ideas as authentic instruction and assessment criteria. Empowers students to explore their own meanings and to perceive the relevance of the domain to their lives (rather than passively accepting meanings from the teacher).
Sandell's FTC Palette ART= Form+ Theme +Context	FORM How is the artwork made?	AESTHETICS/ART HISTORY Is it good art? What does this artwork tell us about the past and present?	THEME What is the artwork about?	CONTEXT When, where, why, and by/for whom was the work created?

Name:_____

SAMPLE ARTMAKING WORKSHEET

Theme: Top 10 things about myself (Self to be or Ideal Self-image)

Medium: Collage—cut-out images and found images from books, magazines, photographs. Scissors and glue stick.

Objectives: Each student will create a multidimensional construct that represents his or her perception of self in collage form. Students will identify 10 qualities related to how she/he perceives herself/himself and what she/he chooses to identify with. This could be a material possession one must have, or values one represents, or things/media that influence what one is and what one wants to be, but first and foremost, how one sees oneself through his or her eyes, or through the reflections they see from others.

Artist Integration: Romare Bearden Collage, Key Artworks: *Watching the Good Trains Go By, 1964; The Block II, 1972*

Art Activity: The final form of the self collage should be carefully planned to achieve the written descriptions, using cut-out images from books or magazines, and make sure to include the following art and design elements:

- A figure that represents yourself head to toe (form/size/proportion)
- A perspective including foreground, middle-ground, and background layers (scale/space/perspective)
- Use of the entire space (composition/balance/unity/color/contrast)
- Use of found images (symbols/words) from books and magazines to represent yourself (Multilayers of Narrative)

Language Arts Integration: Write a self-introduction, including 10 traits that describe you or top 10 things people need to know about you. Then, create a collage to visually represent these 10 qualities you value or want to have. Think of which symbol(s) represents you.

_____

_____

_____

_____

_____

_____

_____

_____

_____

_____

_____

_____

_____

_____

_____

_____

_____

You can think about the following questions that help you begin to germinate your ideas for writing:

- What are you passionate about?
- What inspires you? What does it mean to be a Laker?
- What would you like to become when you grow up?
- What are some world issues you care about and changes you would like to make to improve the world we live in?
- What are some of your goals for the future? Would those be good to write about?
- What sorts of changes, if any, would you like to make in your life?
- What are your relationships with your grandparents, parents, or significant others? What values that your grandparents, parents, or significant others have passed on to you do you most appreciate?
- What are some creative ideas/issues/problems/solutions you want to share with others (e.g., recipes you have prepared together or discovered, or fishing tips you and your father came across during summer vacation on Lake Michigan, etc.)?
- What are some of the things that your grandparents, parents, or significant others have told you that have had an impact on your life or your views, or have changed how you see yourself (My granny told me that I am precious and have a beautiful smile)?

Reflection:

_____

What does this collage say about you? What are some symbols used to represent you?

_____

_____

_____

One new thing I learned about myself while making the artwork was:

_____

_____

One thing you learned about artmaking strategies for classroom activities was:

_____

_____

_____

INTEGRATED CURRICULUM

This section discusses the significance of incorporating visual arts into a K–5 curriculum and a series of related concepts, including the use of big ideas, project-based learning, and integration with other subjects. This integrated approach allows elementary teachers to teach thematically, thereby inspiring curiosity and inviting students to develop their own understandings of the world.

Integrated Curriculum Defined

Beane[29] described curriculum integration as a unifying "whole learning" that connects the contexts of things learned through a student's learning process.[30] Learning is not categorized according to the knowledge of the various subject areas being integrated. Instead, instruction should facilitate meaningful learning in the context of social and personal experiences. This type of whole learning is organized through central ideas (concepts, themes, issues, etc.) that help expand children's understanding of themselves and prepare them for the world they live in. Beane[31] further explained that curriculum integration should include integration of three domains: personal, social, and knowledge:

> First, curriculum is organized around problems and issues that are of personal and social significance in the real world. Second, learning experiences in relation to the organizing center are planned so as to integrate pertinent knowledge in the context of the organizing centers. Third, knowledge is developed and used to address the organizing center currently under study rather than to prepare for some later test or grade level. Finally, emphasis is placed on substantive projects and other activities that involve real application of knowledge, thus increasing the possibility for young people to integrate curriculum experiences into their schemes of meaning and to experience the democratic process of problem solving.[32]

Similarly to Beane's concept of curriculum integration drawn from a child's life as it is being lived and experienced (i.e., interests, experiences, and developments), Efland calls a "life world"[33] where the study of art provides contexts for gaining cognitive inquisitions to develop interpretive forms of inquiry. Parsons[34] and Walker[35] argued that learning in the arts should draw upon knowledge that is relevant to everyday life, and should better reflect the self and social interest and other kinds of knowledge that promote understandings of a broader spectrum of society than do conventional school subjects.

One way to facilitate such inquiry-based "whole learning" is through the use of big ideas—a thematic approach—rather than relying on multi-subject area integration. Stewart and Walker[36] argued that the curriculum should center on big ideas, which serve as a conceptual framework for engaging

[29] James Beane, *Curriculum Integration: Designing the Core of Democratic Education* (New York: Teachers College: Columbia University, 1997).

[30] Ibid., 17.

[31] Ibid.

[32] Ibid., 9.

[33] Efland, *Art and Cognition: Integrting the Visual Arts in the Curriculum*, 121.

[34] Michael Parsons, "Integrated Curriculum and Our Paradigm of Cognition in the Arts," *Studies in Art Education* 39, no. 2 (1998);———, "The Arts and Other Subjects," *Studies in Art Education* 41, no. 3 (2000); Parsons, "The Role of the Visual Arts in the Growth of Mind."

[35] Sydney Walker, "Working in the Black Box: Meaning-Making and Artmaking," *Journal of Art Education* 50, no. 4 (1997);———, *Teaching Meaning in Artmaking*, Art Education in Practice Series. (Worcester, Mass.: Davis Publications, 2001).

[36] Marilyn Stewart and Sydney Walker, *Rethinking Curriculum in Art*, Art Education in Practice Series. (Worcester, Mass.: Davis Publications, 2005); Walker, *Teaching Meaning in Artmaking*.

students in life-centered issues and personal experiences. As Walker[37] pointed out, art should be taught and assessed in meaningfully connected contexts, allowing students to identify themes/ideas that will provide many opportunities for them to connect their life experiences by transferring knowledge across curriculum areas. (See Figure 2.4 for curriculum concept mapping beginning with a central theme).

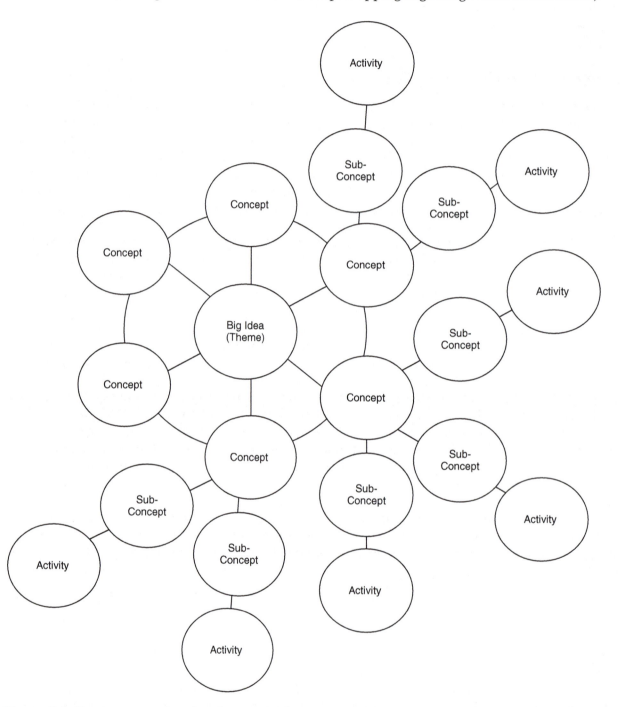

Figure 2.4. Concept mapping for planning a thematic art curriculum using the big idea approach.

[37] Walker, "Working in the Black Box: Meaning-Making and Artmaking.";———, *Teaching Meaning in Artmaking*; Sydney Walker, "What More Can You Ask? Armaking and Inquiry," *Journal of Art Education* 56, no. 5 (2003);——— ———, "Understnding the Artmaking Process: Reflective Practice," *Journal of Art Education* 57, no. 3 (2004);——— —, "How Shall We Teach? Rethinking Artmaking Instruction," *Teaching Artist Journal* 4, no. 3 (2006);———, "Artmaking, Subjectivity, and Signification," *Studies in Art Education* 51, no. 1 (2009).

The Big Idea Approach

Often, art education in elementary education is primarily driven by emotional considerations, or what is termed "creativity"—an approach that can result in students producing little artistic content or in a program with little or no structure—rather than working from an emphasis on the cognitive in art via a conceptually driven approach focusing on *what* to express—the interpretation of ideas and concepts.[38] Historically, the context of learning the arts in the elementary education has focused on techniques, and has placed less emphasis on children's cognitive growth and development. Eisner[39] calls attention to this state of affairs, stressing the unique contributions art could make to children's development in critical and problem solving skills if it were to become a content-oriented discipline. Art has more to offer elementary education, as the key is to encourage elementary teachers to make connections and to conceptualize curriculum instruction within artmaking. To this end, Stewart and Walker[40] suggest that the development of the art curriculum should begin with a central theme that develops knowledge. This type of conceptual framework is called "big ideas." Walker[41] defines big ideas as enduring ideas—umbrella themes based on relationships to the meanings and values of people's daily lives. They are similar to themes, topics, or issues that investigate human existence:

> [Big ideas]—broad, important human issues—are characterized by complexity, ambiguity, contradiction, and multiplicity. Whether stated as single terms, phrases, or compete statements, big ideas do not completely explicate an idea, but represent a host of concepts that form the idea. For example, the term conflict may represent a number of concepts, such as power, personal and social values, justice and injustice, and winners and losers.[42]

When teaching using art, Walker argues that the big ideas (such as identity, power, relationships, life cycles, change, ritual, human and nature, etc.) approach can foster conceptual thinking and meaningful artmaking relevant to students' lives rather than trying to force artistic growth and creative endeavor. Art educator McFee[43] addressed the importance of teaching art within cultural contexts; Brent Wilson[44] goes further to argue that the art curriculum should also include the interests of students, reflecting their cultures and connecting to their real-world experiences.

Therefore, the art curriculum ought to reflect the values of cultures and cultural diversity; art instruction should connect to students' lives and provide a context for understanding culture, issues of power, history, and self-identity.[45] As art educators, therefore, we should help students "create meaning and understanding of their lives in the present and imagine possibilities for their lives in the future" by emphasizing "cultural production and investigation of images and artifacts."[46] When planning a curriculum, instructors should focus on inquiry (conceptual

[38] Walker, "What More Can You Ask? Armaking and Inquiry."

[39] Eisner, *The Arts and Creation of Mind.*

[40] Stewart and Walker, *Rethinking Curriculum in Art*; Walker, *Teaching Meaning in Artmaking.*

[41] Walker, *Teaching Meaning in Artmaking.*

[42] Ibid., 1.

[43] June King McFee and Rogena M. Degge, *Art, Culture, and Environment : A Catalyst for Teaching* (Dubuque, Iowa: Kendall/Hunt Pub. Co., 1980).

[44] Brent Wilson, "The Superherroes of J.C. Holz:Plus and Outline of a Theory of Child Art," *Journal of Art Education* 27, no. 8 (1974);———, "Figure Structure, Figure Action, and Framing in the Drawings of American and Egyptian Children." *Studies in Art Education* 21, no. 1 (1979);———, "Of Diagrams and Rhizomes: Visual Culture, Contemporary Art, and the Impossibility of Mapping the Content of Art Education," *Studies of Art Education* 3, no. 44 (2003);———, "Child Art after Modernism: Visual Culture and New Narratives," in *Handbook of Research and Policy in Art Education* ed. Elliot Eisner and Michael Day (NJ: Mahwah: Lawrence Erlbaum., 2004); Wilson and Toku, "Boys' Love, *Yaoi*, and Art Education: Issues of Power and Pedagogy."

[45] Christine Ballengee-Morris and Patricia Stuhr, "Multicultural Art and Visual Cultural Education in a Changing World," *Journal of Art Education* 54, no. 4 (2001).

[46] Ibid.: 6.

thinking) and the interpretive purpose (symbolic meanings) as ways for students to express their ideas related to personal and cultural meaning.

Daniel and Stuhr[47] provides a variety of methods by which teachers may integrate big ideas and apply integrated-thinking pedagogy to classroom art instruction. They explain that big ideas and key concepts must be relevant to students' lives. When adapting a big idea in curriculum planning, it should be considered at two levels—both generally and as to its significance and relevance to the needs and interests of the students. To integrate big ideas into the K–5 curriculum, the unit foundation should include themes (or big ideas) key concepts, and essential questions to promote integrated thinking and provide an understanding of the curriculum the students can relate to. Brainstorming is another way to generate key concepts and essential questions. If the big idea is a theme, then key concepts are the topics that underlie this theme (see student sample unit planning on pages 75–79).

Project-based Learning through the Big Idea Approach

An example of the community as a big idea is provided in Daniel and Stuhr's analysis of a celebration of the African American community and culture—"the Kwanzaa playground."[48] In the article, Daniel and Stuhr show how the community serves as a theme for the unit's big idea in teaching students about the importance of relationships in one's community and the importance of visual arts in promoting social betterment through celebration. Essential questions challenge each student to explore the characteristics of his or her own *community* and the role of art in that community (Social Studies, Language Arts Connection).

Community as a Big Idea: Daniel, Stuhr and Walker encourage teachers to explore essential questions when planning a curriculum.[49] Essential questions are initiators of creative and critical thinking. In other words, essential questions are those that drive the lesson's big idea. By asking questions, students have to think critically to answer issues confronting them. For example, if community is a big idea for the unit lesson, the essential questions can be:[50]

> How is a community defined?
> What kinds of places can be found in communities?
> What values does your community reflect?

These questions not only connect to students' prior knowledge but also scaffold what they need to know. The community serves as a big idea that is relevant to student's lives and thus can be easily integrated into multiple contexts of learning. For example, in connecting with the language arts, students learn to define *community* (or *neighborhood*); students respond to an example of art in the community and recognize that a community is formed when a group of people work together for a common goal or value. Students can learn what it means to be a community member, and students can put the activity in action by helping or giving service in the community (see Figure 2.5).

In planning a studio activity with a language arts connection, the curriculum and instruction should also aim to teach an understanding that integrates the student's learning process. For younger children, the activity can begin by asking students if they know what a community is, then asking students to describe and write about places in their communities and to sketch out each place being identified (see Figure 2.6). Doing so would be a way of gauging students'

---

[47] Vasta Daniel and Patricia Stuhr, "Suggestions for Integrating the Arts into Curriculum," *Journal of Art Education* 59, no. 1 (2006).
[48] Ibid.
[49] Ballengee-Morris and Stuhr, "Multicultural Art and Visual Cultural Education in a Changing World."; Daniel and Stuhr, "Suggestions for Integrating the Arts into Curriculum."; Walker, *Teaching Meaning in Artmaking*.
[50] Further discussion see Daniel and Stuhr, "Suggestions for Integrating the Arts into Curriculum."

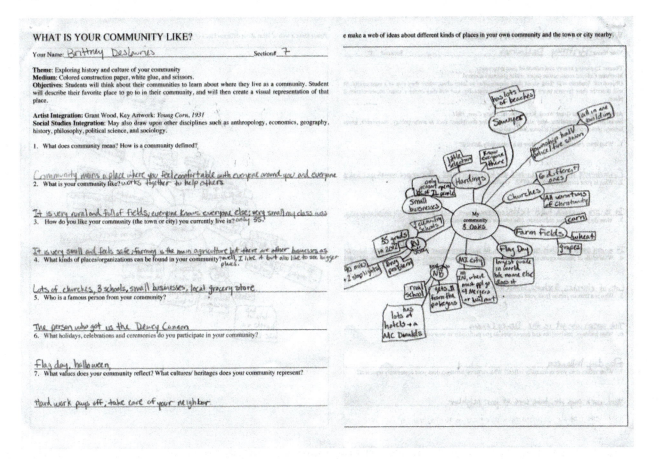

Figure 2.5. In-class worksheet for brainstorming about favorite places in the community, including in-class worksheet for defining a community, geographic concept mapping of the community, from city communities to the state level. Images used permission by student artist, Brittney DesLauries.

understanding. Daniel and Stuhr[51] point out that *brainstorming* is an important scaffolding strategy that allows students to make connections with what they know (prior knowledge). It is necessary that students brainstorm about the community and make a web of ideas about special places in the community. This concept mapping serves an interpretive purpose and allows for meaning-making in relation to the larger social world, connecting what students already know to what they might know about communities geographically (see Figure 2.5).

To create meaningful art activities, curriculum goals should teach for an understanding that relates art to the world. One way to integrate the community theme with art is to incorporate artists whose work has the community theme as a subject (see student sample lesson planning). For example, Grant Wood, an American painter whose work was much invested in the figurative painting of rural American themes, often took his subjects from his hometown, including the use of farmers, memories of his childhood, and people he knew from the community. Wood is well known for his regionalist paintings that depict the rural American Midwest farmlands and farmworkers. By learning about an artist such as Wood, students learn about the value of the community he painted, as well as his artmaking strategies and the concept of the community as an inspiration for artmaking (see Figure 2.7). One way to expand students' knowledge and thinking is to ask them to explore the value of their community represented, inviting them to ask questions of what they see, and feel about their community, and how they can make a difference in their community. (For more themes and a list of possible artists to integrate please see Walker's Chapter 8 in *Rethinking Curriculum in Art.*)

[51] Ibid.

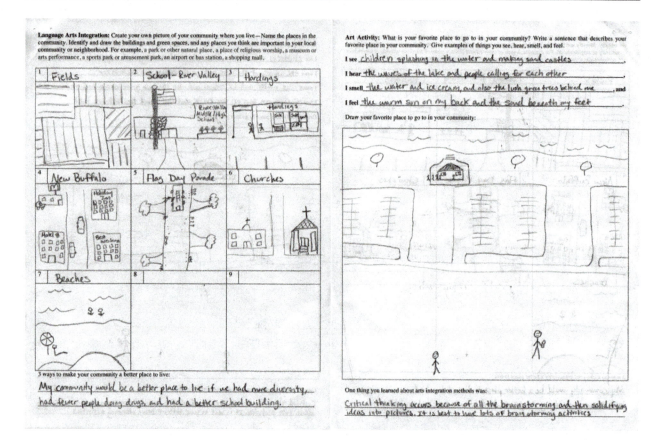

Figure 2.6. In-class worksheet for brainstorming about favorite places in the community, including in-class worksheet for brainstorming about places in the community, and a final sketch for a favorite place to go to in community. Images used permission by student artist, Brittney DesLauries.

Figure 2.7. Close-up images of student work in the medium of collage, using community as the theme. The project asked students to render their favorite place to go to (Michigan as an example). Image used permission by student artists, Brittney DesLauries [Left] and Emily Kummer [Right].

SAMPLE LESSON PLAN: Student Example-Community as the Theme

Unit 1-Community
Unit Title: Exploring Hometown Values with Hokusai
Grade Level: 4th
Used with permission of the student, Brandon West

Lesson Overview:
Hokusai's woodblock prints of various Japanese landscapes tell us about his culture and his values. By examining his artwork, we can learn how to look at our own environments, specifically our hometowns, and see what we value. By comparing and contrasting our societal values to those of Hokusai, we can begin a dialogue about cultural differences. This dialogue will contribute to our appreciation and understanding of others' experience.

Big Idea (Theme): Community

Key Concept:
- A community is formed by a group of people who work together to achieve a common goal or who share a similar value.

Essential Question
- How does your hometown influence the values you have?

Objectives:
- Students will begin to identify their personal and community values.
- Students will recognize how living in their hometown shapes the way they perceive the world.
- Students will be able to identify artwork by Hokusai.
- Students will begin to understand how every culture has different values.

Area of Integration: Art, Language Arts, and Social Studies
Selected Artist: Katsushika Hokusai
Hokusai is one of Japan's most famous artists. He is best known for his woodblock prints, which depict landscapes and people from Japan. Ironically, Hokusai's artwork is not traditionally Japanese. His nontraditional art style is influenced by Dutch and French art. His work also breaks Japanese traditions because it depicts the "average" man and not rich people or heroes. These landscapes tell us about Hokusai and the Japanese culture.

Appreciation of beauty is part of the Japanese character. Zen Buddhism and the Shinto religion have influenced many works of art. We can see an appreciation of nature in Japanese paintings, statues, pottery, and even gardens. In other styles of art we can see an appreciation for Japanese history and for popular heroes of the time. The appreciation of nature is apparent in Hokusai's work. His landscapes tell us what he values, which has been influenced by his connection to Japan. Looking at Hokusai's work allows us to reflect on his values, which are shown through his art, as well as our own values in our own hometowns.

Artist: Hokusai
Key Artwork: Big wave, Selected Prints from *36 Years on Mount Fuji*, Ancient Pontoon Bridge, Kameido Tenjin Shrine

Artmaking Strategies: Wood Block Printing, Painting, Japanese landscapes influenced by Chinese and Western styles.

Related Studio Activity:
Students will be doing a mono-printing activity. Mono-printing is very similar to the woodblock printing style Hokusai used. Thus, students will imitate the style of the artist. They will draw their own

hometowns on Styrofoam board. This activity will allow them to reflect on their personal values and those of their community and to examine these.

Key Ideas:
- How our hometowns reflect personal and community values.
- How culture influences our values (e.g., Western art vs. Japanese art)
- Creating art that reflects an important value you have.

Sub Ideas:
- How is your social life affected by your hometown?
- In what ways are your emotional needs met by your community?
- How does the economic situation of your hometown affect you?
- Geography: Relative location of hometown

Preparation before Art Project:
Before the Art Project, the teacher will:
- Research the artist and locate resources that will aid in the creation of the lesson.
- Choose a key concept and create a lesson.
- The teacher will devise any necessary PowerPoint presentations and hand-outs for students.
- The teacher will locate and obtain all necessary materials necessary for the studio project.

Procedure for Art Lesson:

First Day
- The teacher will introduce the artist through a PowerPoint presentation.
- The teacher will facilitate a discussion about concepts discussed in the lesson.
- Students will think about their hometowns and how they have been shaped by them. They will then answer the questions on the worksheet.
- Students will create a sketch of their mono-print.

Second Day
- The teacher will recap day one's events.
- The students will sketch their drawing onto the Styrofoam board, and then carve the lines.
- The students will choose colors of ink and construction paper for their mono-prints.
- The students will create two or three mono-prints.

Third Day
- The teacher will have students show their mono-prints to their classmates.
- The teacher will facilitate a discussion about their artwork.
- The students will reflect on Hokusai's artwork and their own. They will observe both similarities and differences.

Resources and Materials:
- PowerPoint presentation
- The text: *One Day in Japan with Hokusai*, Prestel Publishing
- Computer/Internet access
- Styrofoam board, ink rollers, Plexiglas

- Pens/Pencils
- Worksheets
- Ink
- Construction paper

Vocabulary:
- **Values**: Concepts that describe the beliefs of an individual or culture.
- **Perception**: The way we view the world based on our experiences, location, and relationships.
- **Culture**: the customary beliefs, social forms, and material traits of a racial, religious, or social group.

Follow-up Activity:
Once students exhibit an understanding of the essential question, they will choose an artist from a region of the world connected to their cultural heritage. For this project, they will look at three to four key pieces of artwork and formulate a thesis about what they notice. Based on that thesis, they will write a one-page paper discussing what they think the artwork says about their artist's personal and cultural values. Once students present and revise their papers through a writer's workshop, they will then formally research their chosen artist. They will then present their findings to the class, detailing what they have observed and discovered through their research.

The Sample Rubric for Student Evaluation: Community

Lesson Goals/Points	4 Excellent	3 Good	2 Poor	1 Not Accepted
Displays understanding of key concept	Is able to identify key concepts and answer essential questions	Can accurately identify most of the key concepts/essential questions	Can identify one or two of the key concepts/Partially understands the essential question	Little or no progress in identifying aspects of other cultures
Demonstrates competency in key concept	Is able to accurately explain the concepts taught to other students	Is able to explain the concepts taught to other students at a basic level	Struggles to explain the concepts learned to other students	Cannot accurately understand the concepts on his or her own.
Can apply the techniques taught in class to other activities throughout the unit	Uses application techniques to do extended practice activities	Understands application techniques but struggles to apply some of them	Understands some application ideas but struggles to apply them	Does not understand techniques or know how to apply them
Completion of project involved with content area instruction	Completed the project accurately and in a timely fashion	Completed the project in a timely fashion with a few mistakes	Did not complete the entire project	Turned in less than 50 percent of the project
Participation	Participated in all the activities completely	Missed one activity in class	Missed over half of the activities	Participated in none of the activities

Concept Mapping:

Key Concept Map:

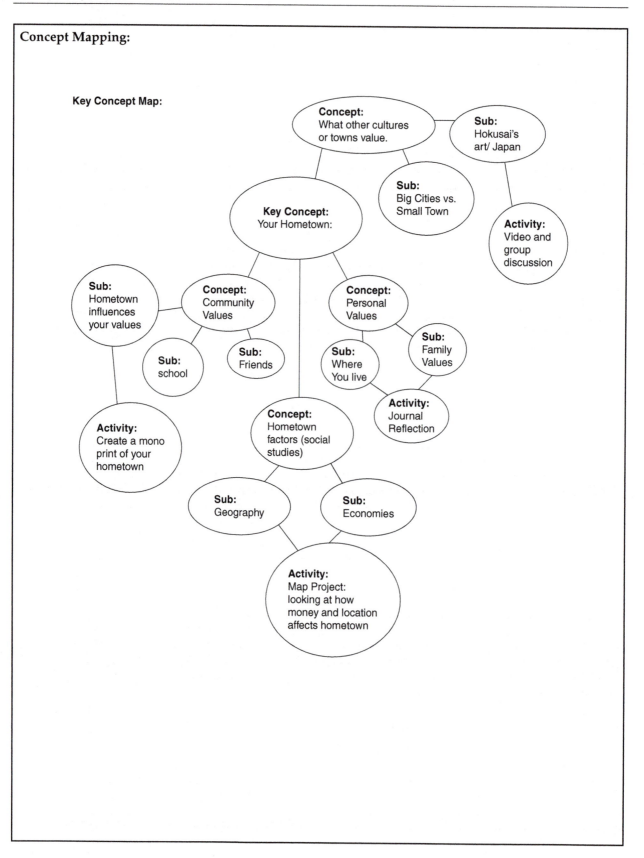

Hometown Mono-Printing

Name:_____

COMMUNITY WORKSHEET FOR ARTMAKING

Hokusai's woodblock-print landscapes reflect certain values that both he and his fellow Japanese found important, such as the importance of nature. Now, it's your turn to think about your values. Values are things you strongly believe in and shape the way you act. For example, if I come from a small town, I might value the sense of community. If I were to draw my hometown based on this value, it would probably show people working and playing together outside their households.

Name one or two values you that are important to you.

What values does your hometown reflect?

How are your values influenced by your hometown?

Now, sketch your mono-print!

- Key Artwork:_____
- Key Ideas:_____
- Key Art-making Strategies:_____
- Art Medium:_____

Group Discussion:

Brainstorm studio activities to develop student's art-making based on the artist researched above. Please provide worksheets for guiding students' development of their ideas through creative expression, delving into questions requiring conceptual understanding through exploring, questioning, and problematizing the big idea (issues, ideas, concepts) *through art-making.* You should consider such questions as

- What is the conceptual focus (issues/concepts) for engaging students in art-making based on the study of the artist? What is the subject for art-making (self-portrait, community building, me in an ideal place, etc.)?

- What are some of the artist's art-making strategies that will help students work out their ideas through personal expression? What is the technical problem for engaging students in art-making? What art medium will students learn about and use to create their art (drawing, watercolors, crayons, clay, etc.)?

- What are some methods for integrating art with other subject areas? For example, writing skills can be practiced through having students describe, interpret, judge, and analyze a piece of artwork; mathematical skills can be reinforced by having students count, add, or subtract shapes; social studies can be taught by having students investigate context; history can be engaged by studying artistic inventions that have shaped history; science can be incorporated, such as by having students depict the animal kingdom food web and food chain.

GUIDELINES FOR CREATING A VISUAL ART LESSON PLAN

As a group, you will design one lesson plan that integrates visual arts with elementary education based on a specific grade level. The required portions for the visual arts should include a visual curriculum and art activity that teaches a big idea (selected theme), incorporating one contemporary artist as a teaching instrument. The lesson should include a big idea and key concepts that delve into the deeper meanings and questions related to themes of human existence (i.e., relationship, power, fantasy/dream, diversity, change, celebration, identity).

LESSON GUIDELINES

Names of Group Members:

Lesson Title (Be Descriptive):

Grade Level:

Area(s) of Integration:

1. LESSON OVERVIEW
What is it you are going to teach? Why is this important? (teacher reflection; significance of the lesson outcome; rationale; and purpose of the lesson)

2. OBJECTIVE AND BENCHMARK (MICHIGAN STATE VISUAL ARTS STANDARDS AND BENCHMARKS) (ex. ART.I.VA.EL.1)
List specifically what you want students to learn, what students will be able to do at the end of the lesson, and how they can apply it. How will it be measured/observed? For example, upon the completion of the course, students will…

3. ART CONTENT KNOWLEDGE/ARTIST/ART-MAKING STRATEGY/ART ACTIVITY
    BIG IDEA (theme):
    KEY CONCEPT(S) (state as a statement):
    ESSENTIAL QUESTION(S) (state as a question):
    SELECTED ARTIST:
    • Please provide contextual information about the artist:
    • Key artwork:
    • Art-making strategies:
    ART ACTIVITY:
    • Description of the art activity:
    • Key ideas:
    • Sub ideas:
    BRAINSTORMING RELATED STUDIO ACTIVITY:
    • Choice of media, subject matter, formal limitations:
    • Personal connections:
    • Development of student ideas for expression:
    CONCEPT MAPPING: Please provide a map that illustrates how you will teach the big idea (theme) or understand the key concept.

4. ANTICIPATORY SET
    RESOURCES AND MATERIALS:
    List everything you will need for the lesson, including visuals, materials, and books.
    List what needs to be done before the lesson begins.

PROCEDURE AND PREPARATION FOR ART LESSON:
List the basic steps involved during the lesson. (If the activity involves more than one segment of time, indicate Day 1, Day 2, etc.)

VOCABULARY:
Two to five key words (provide definition for each term).

5. SPECIAL NEEDS ADAPTATIONS
   - This art project is specifically designed to be adapted for students with a _____ disability (may be multiple disabilities).
   - Provide definition of the disability.
   - Identify characteristics of the disability. Please identify student behaviors and skills, strengths and weaknesses associated with the disability.
   - Identify your goals, core concepts, skills, and materials needed for the project to be completed by students.
   - Outline your instructions and strategies for completing the art activity in steps.
   - List adaptations and modifications to be incorporated in the curriculum for inclusion of students with the disability.

6. ASSESSMENT/EVALUATION/RUBRICS
   Briefly list the expected student competencies and methods you will use to evaluate student learning outcome. What evidence do I have that the students learned the objectives? Describe the task or performance that students will be evaluated on your rubric.

7. CLOSURE AND FOLLOW-UP (student wrap-up; lesson summary)
   List exit questions and activities that further reinforce the objectives and content. These may be interdisciplinary.

8. WORKSHEET(S) FOR GUIDING STUDENT ART-MAKING AND EXAMPLE(S) OF ART ACTIVITY PRODUCTION
   Please provide worksheet(s) and an example of this intended lesson outcome (e.g., photo of your own creation).

Rubric for Grading an Art Lesson Plan

Grading Criteria	
	Lesson Plan: Develop instructional lessons that integrate visual arts into elementary curriculum and that also meet the Michigan Arts Education Content Standards.
	BASICS: Clarity of lesson and components follow the guidelines. Uses an artist to teach big idea and engages students with key concepts using essential questions. Clearly states a list of objectivities, materials, preparations, and procedures. Provides activities and rubrics for evaluating student learning processes and outcomes.

(Continued)

Rubric for Grading an Art Lesson Plan (Continued)	
A Exemplary	Exemplary lesson, well designed and integrated. Shows a holistic understanding about using visual artist to teach big ideas and key concepts and engages students with essential questions. Lesson is complete and easy to follow. Excellent, well-thought-out. Shows holistic approach to understanding about culture(s). Provides activities, worksheets to document student learning outcomes, using rubrics. Visual example attached; well exemplified with high quality.
B Accomplished	Accomplished. Lesson shows a good understanding of arts integration using artist to teach a big idea, relevant key concepts, and engages students with good essential questions. Lesson is mostly complete and/or easy to follow, integrates artist's art-making, and includes a rubric to assess student's learning outcome and provides activity.
C Developing	Developing. Average lesson shows little understanding of arts integration, using the artist to teach a relevant big idea, provides a few key concepts and use of essential questions for discussion. Lesson shows some understanding of arts integration and little engagement of the art-making process.
D Beginning	Unorganized, poorly designed, large parts are incomplete and/or inaccurate. Difficult to follow. Weak big idea/key concepts. Lesson shows little understanding about using the artist to teach concepts or engage students with essential questions. No rubric; no activity.
F Unacceptable	Lesson plan incomplete, incorrect, and/or inadequate. Lesson plan shows little or no theme/key concept related to the artist at all. No rubric.

CHINESE DRAGONS IN AN AMERICAN SCIENCE UNIT

LEE YUEN LEW AND JOHN W. McLURE

Can art and science find a happy home in the same unit? We think the answer is yes, if the central problem interests the students and allows them to try out multiple abilities.

The sixth-grade unit described in this article, which we called "The Dragon Project," grew mainly from two roots, a study of ancient China and a later probe into anatomy and physiology. The host institution was Ross School, located in East Hampton, New York. This campus-style exploratorium is noted for its interdisciplinary studies based on a humanistic core of world cultures. By "interdisciplinary studies" we are referring to problem solving that uses input from several subjects in a way that interests students more than traditional methods and content do (Walker, 2003). In this unit, aesthetics fueled the problem solving.

The inspiration for The Dragon Project began with an exhibition in the Seattle Museum of East Asian Art. In the exhibition, a placard depicted a Qing Dynasty (1644–1912) recipe/formula for painting dragons and included a hybrid animal with a camel's head, deer horns, rabbit eyes, cow ears, snake neck, frog belly, carp scales, hawk claws, and tiger palms. By the time of the Emperor Qin Long, who was approximately a contemporary of George Washington, a rule prohibited any nobles from wearing dragon designs that showed as many as five claws. That number was reserved for the emperor only.

Roughly one and one-half centuries before the Qing Dynasty, Leonardo da Vinci was puzzling over representations of fantastic creatures, including dragons. He wrote, "Take for its head that of a mastiff or setter, for its eyes those of a cat, for its ears those of a porcupine, for its nose that of a greyhound, with the eyebrows of a lion, the temples of an old cock, and the neck of a water tortoise" (MacCurdy, 1955). Da Vinci illustrated a smooth-skinned dragon with bat wings, along with the rest of his formula (Zubov, 1968). By contrast, the artists whose works appear in the Seattle Museum deviated from the Qing formula.

A second artistic inspiration for the Dragon Project comes from playing with fantastic creatures. These creatures are found in children's books with split pages that encourage viewers to combine animal parts randomly with hilarious results. See Sarah Ball's (1985) book *Porguacan*, for instance.

Another example is found in Jean Fisher's review of the art objects of Joan Fontcuberta and Pere Formiguera, based on the doubtful discoveries of Professor Peter Ameisenhaufen ("Anthill"). One of Ameisenhaufen's finds is "*Hermaphrotaurus autositarius*, an androgynous, carnivorous bovine, eight-legged, double-bodied, and single-headed, whose male part continually sleeps unless the insomniac female part wakes it to mate" (Fisher, 1988).

Meanwhile, we were facing an exploration of anatomy/physiology in the third trimester. We felt that we could begin with a study of systems based on the human body and end with an exercise in comparative anatomy with a description of the dragon as the central project.

Our underlying philosophy is grounded in constructivism. We think that a conception makes more lasting sense to students if they construct most of the meaning themselves based on personal experience. That construction involves hands-on creation (Brooks & Brooks, 1993; Phillips, 1995; Yager, 1991, 2000). Visual arts engage students in problem solving activities that help them to develop cognitive, affective, and psychomotor skills to select and transform ideas, discriminate, synthesize, and appraise. The Dragon Project is a perfect vehicle for developing and using these skills; the project allows students to experience innovative ways of communicating their thoughts, ideas, and visions—an ideal of artistic expression.

We envisioned a Dragon Project that would move through several stages. We would begin with a discussion of dragons followed by a first impression (generation) illustration. Next, there would be library and Internet research to expand student knowledge and open up new, more complex design possibilities. Eventually, the students were to move into two- or three-dimensional constructions, whose anatomy they had to define either individually or in groups. We hoped that some students might make Power-Point™ presentations to accompany their dragon.

We worked out a rubric for a three-dimensional work that contained more points and an embedded challenging problem. Could students explain and design the organ in a dragon that produces smoke and fire?

"WHY SCIENCE, WHY DO IT AT ALL, HOW WILL THIS HELP ME?"

The beginning rubric (see Figure 1) soon felt too procrustean, even in the planning stage. We wanted larger possibilities for the expansion of learning to include the dragon's life cycle, to specify at least five internal organs and their functions in a particular system, and to encourage the construction of a PowerPoint presentation that would summarize the entire project for those students who worked in pairs or small groups. Eventually, all students created PowerPoint presentations. Aesthetic appeal also emerged as a larger factor than our initial rubric could handle. We found so much charm in the first generation illustrations that they overwhelmed our scoring system.

Initial Impressions and Student Perceptions of Dragons Across the Globe

Da Vinci found a challenge in illustrating fantastic creatures and we still felt this challenge with the dragon. There is a creative ambiguity—some might say cognitive dissonance—that was increased by our science classroom setting.

Some students were evidently surprised. In the end, there were refreshing comments, skepticisms, and sighs of relief from the students that the project was not so intimidating after all. In addition, there were revelations that various cultures have such different views of dragons.

	Points	
	2-Dimensional Design	**3-Dimensional Design**
References Used (1 point for the reference, 1 point per Xerox™ copy used)	N	N
Aesthetic Appeal, overall (opinion of teacher or outside judges)	1-10	1-20
One point for each animal body part used accurately in the design, with no limit on the number of animals. A particular species of animal may only be used once, so that one could use a bear's claws and teeth, but would get credit for one animal. Thus, the Qing Dynasty recipe design could gain a maximum score of 30 if only one reference book was used (2 points for one reference used, 18 points for 9 body parts, and 10 for aesthetic appeal). Some energetic students may double this score.	1-N	1-N

Figure 1. Initial rubric.

When I first heard about this project I thought, "Why science, why do it at all, how will this help me?" Also, "I figured there would be nothing on dragons so I thought it [research] would be very hard, almost too hard to do. Once I went online, I had too much to choose from! Then, I thought building my dragon would be impossible! Of course, it wasn't!" (Meaghan, personal communication, Spring 2003).

When we first started, I was thinking to myself, "What do dragons have to do with science?" But when we got more into the project, I understood that the dragon's anatomy (bone structure, systems, etc.) was very scientific. (Antonia, personal communication, Spring 2003)

I was surprised at how many dragons [there] are in different cultures. (Alayah, personal communication, Spring 2003)

I learned that unlike the Western perceptions of a big, mean dragon, many Eastern countries believe dragons are good luck and kind. (Jasper, personal communication, Spring 2003)

Evolution of Students' Conceptions of Dragon from First Generation Drawings to Second Generation Drawings to 3-D Models

The students' views of dragons evolved from prior conceptions (first generation drawings) through the early research phase of the unit, to second generation drawings, and finally to the full dragon models. In general, we found three categories in student drawings. Three out of a total of 24 students drew very elaborate, detailed first generation dragons. These perceptions generally did not change much by the end of their unit (i.e., their second generation dragon was an almost exact replica of their first). Incidentally, the dragons built by these students usually did not resemble their ideas. Could it be that these students found it difficult to build in accordance with the highly complex structures envisioned? The majority of the students, however, showed increased details, labeled parts and identified borrowings from other animals. Part of the development seemed to be associated with exposure to such varied animalistic forms found in diverse cultures. Several students (5 out of 24) put little or no color into their initial drawings of dragons. Generally, these same students expressed difficulty with drawing a dragon out of their imagination. They stressed that although they had heard of, read of, and seen many different dragon pictures in books, movies, and TV, they just could not draw a dragon with confidence or visualize what color it would take. They felt that their ideas were "too fuzzy." These same students are the ones whose second generation dragons took on vast contrasts from their initial drawings.

Our overall impression is that the first generation drawings showed high spontaneous creativity. The second generation drawings represented a step back to lower or different creativity as students reintegrated the new impressions of the dragon. The third generation models showed another high creativity phase, maybe the richest numerically, since they produced more kinds of organs and aspects of the beasts which then had to be explained.

When students create a working model of their dragon, they are in a sense creating an extension of themselves/their own bodies and viewing their expression in a new and different environment. Through the process of artistic creation we develop our own identity and give voice to our inner thoughts, feelings, and ideas. This goal is achieved by first imagining and then finally creating a fantastic creature placed in a suitable life sustaining, aesthetically pleasing as well as culturally and historically accurate environment.

In the students' early conceptions of dragons, three categories emerged: "friendly/neutral," "evil/violent," and "big/powerful," along with two comments that appeared to require classifications of a simpler sort, "traditional" and "divergent." Some double classifying also occurred. The comments fell roughly into the evil/violent category about as often as they did into the friendly/neutral. The traditional and divergent categories were also about equal.

We anticipated that the various cultural interpretations of dragons would feed impressions of hugeness and male violence, and that the rubric would encourage deviation from the Qing

Evil/Violent Dragons	Big/Powerful Dragons	Friendly/Neutral Dragons
It was evil, really bad —Larissa A dragon is a winged beast —Pierre ...feared by all other sea creatures —Jasper Vicious, mythical beasts that crave for the blood of others —Daniel	Feared by all —Jasper Dragons, mythical creatures with a great power —Ashley To me the dragon is a sign of power, god and wit. Power because they are big and strong. Godly because they are a sign of mercy. Wit because in old times, dragons were signs of bravery —AG	I think a dragon can be friendly or mean —Katie I think dragons are good unless provoked. They may be dangerous or may be gentle —Ashley

Figure 2. Students' early perceptions of dragons.

Dynasty recipe. The latter appeared to happen, although we cannot say why. Yet, we did not anticipate the appearance of friendly, even beautiful dragon imagery, as in the case of the butterfly version. Some of the student comments are listed in Figure 2.

In the student reflections about their later dragon concepts (second generation), we saw much more clarification of the animal's characteristics. Even those who did not yet name the parts to be borrowed felt that the newer version was different. The students directed less attention toward the larger, dramatic first impressions (big, scary, violent, friendly) and the tone was cooler, more rational.

The student comments on the building phase also differed from those of earlier stages. We sensed more concentration on the process of construction perhaps due to the many demands for problem-solving. When a need arose, the builder could find an artifact or body part, depending on the natural model. One student found that spoons would serve as flippers.

... we started building off this metal basket. That's when we figured out to make our dragon aquatic, so we used spoons for its hands so it could swim faster. (Charlie, personal communication, Spring 2003)

The dragon that my group made was based from chicken wire. We used wrapping paper smooshed up for the head and wrapping paper rolls for the tail. (Ashley, personal communication, Spring 2003)

National Education Standards: Visual Arts Content Standards (grades 4–8) and Science Content Standard C (grades 5–8)

Visual Arts Content Standard 4: "Understanding the visual arts in relation to history & culture" (MENC, 1994, p. 50) can be addressed in the study of various societal and cultural definitions and visualizations of dragons as symbols, myths, and omens of good or evil based on particular cultural beliefs and practices throughout history. The visual arts offer the richness of drawing and painting, sculpture, and design, all of which are incorporated into The Dragon Project. Imagination is also an important part of making art. This project allows students to delve into their imaginative selves as they combine their knowledge of science, culture, history and literature to create their dragon models, in which case Content Standard 6 "Making connections between visual arts and other disciplines" (MENC, 1994, p. 51) comes into play.

Student learning with respect to "Science Content Standard C (5–8) Life Science: Structure and function in living systems, diversity and adaptations of organisms," (MENC, 1994, p. 155) was evident through different stages of the Dragon Project. We were struck by the similarity of this statement to the details in Visual Arts Content Standard 2: "Using Knowledge of Structures and Functions," which is employed in the designing and building of the dragon.

The wrap-up occurred during the students' final presentations when students defended their dragon taxonomy. Over 50% of the students believed their dragon to be a mix of reptile (many likening it to a lizard) and bird. There were other mixtures of dual taxonomy, but a majority of the dragons fell into categories of reptile, bird, and fish, in that order. Other students thought there were links to mammals and even amphibians.

A vast majority of students also believed that their dragons lived both on land and in water, and connected these habitats to their dragons' lungs and gills, respectively. On the other hand, there were those students whose dragons lived only on land and had only lungs, as well as those which lived solely in the water and had only gills, but were equipped with fins and air floats for swimming. Most students also believed that their dragons were omnivorous and connected the dragon's digestive system to that of humans. There were also references to teeth structures used for eating meat and plants.

Students also demonstrated a range of knowledge with regard to whether their dragons were poikilotherms (cold-blooded) or homiotherms (warm-blooded), or whether their dragons laid eggs or had live babies (mammals). Students drew charts of suggested life cycles and portrayed them in PowerPoint presentations.

Finally, students met the criteria for Visual Arts Content Standard 5: "Reflecting upon and assessing the characteristics and merits of their work and the work of others" in a wonderful display and exhibit of their dragons. This exhibition emphasized the importance of sharing one's artwork with others as well as giving and receiving criticism necessary for understanding and growth.

In addition to the four Standards in Visual Arts and that of Science Standard Content C, this interdisciplinary project addressed at least three other Science Standards and Standards in World History and Technology.

DISCUSSION

The students seemed to understand that their work had evolved in stages. Perhaps they felt that their bigger, complex, three-dimensional models were necessarily superior to the initial, light, breezy designs. One wrote,

> All of our second generation dragons came out a lot better than our first generation dragons. They were more detailed, labeled, elaborate, and descriptive. When you compare my two pictures (first and second generation dragons), they remain the same shape, (but) they are very different. (Meaghan, personal communication, Spring 2003)

We felt that some of the final dragon constructions were not as aesthetically appealing as several of the first generation drawings, even though the models required more effort. We sensed an irresistible spontaneity in them, a sense of unrestrained expression. For example, where did the ephemeral "butterfly dragon" go? Had we unconsciously ignored Elkins's (1999) warning, "Pictures are the strongest agents for the corruption of meaning" (p. 240)? Even though Elkins was referring to a dichotomy of pictures and text, we wondered if the resolution of the cognitive dissonance eliminated some of the "dragon-ness."

Did the students grasp the interdisciplinary connections in the unit? We think the answer is affirmative. Ashley, a pert sixth grader, wrote,

> Although this project was based on a fictional creature, we added a lot of knowledge from cultural history, technology, art, and science into our dragon. We learned that the Chinese worshipped and loved their dragons, unlike the Japanese who hate and are afraid of their dragons. Our studies from technology helped with our PowerPoint presentation. We made

organs out of all grey clay and took (digital) pictures of them. We put the digital pictures in Adobe Photoshop Elements™ to change the lighting and color of the organs to make them more realistic. We used our knowledge of PowerPoint to make a huge part of our presentation. We used our knowledge of art to build the organs and the dragon itself. The science I learned was our knowledge of organs which we researched on the Internet and our knowledge of the dragon's taxonomy. I think that this project was so fun because dragons are fictional, but I learned science, art, technology . . . all from this project. I think it's great that I learned so much from integrated studies." (Ashley, personal communication, Spring 2003)

Both during the unit and in retrospect, we saw interplay between various disciplines.

CONCLUSION

The Dragon Project began in the discipline of art, in class discussion, and in the first impression illustrations. As the students expanded their knowledge of dragons through library and Internet research, the learning reached into mythology, societal customs, and paleontology, regarding possible connections between dinosaur bones and dragon stories. The three-dimensional dragon construction stage pushed the students into a blend of art and science (anatomy and physiology). Materials, colors, and textures were applied within the taxonomic choices that the students made. If the beast was part amphibian, how could they make a slimy skin? Should they line the esophagus with a heat shield to protect the animal against its own fire?

Our students rose to the challenge to build their dragons. Most took their work home where parents and siblings helped out. The final models brought families to school to view the bestiary. Several gave rave reactions.

We plan to repeat the unit. To interested teachers, we submit these recommendations:

- Use a project method that allows plenty of student choice;
- Allow the project to represent a new set of challenges;
- Base the unit on constructivism, on the personal experiences of the students;
- Encourage the students to present and defend their dragon designs using PowerPoint;
- Ground the unit in appropriate educational standards;
- Use a flexible rubric in your evaluation;
- Probe the characteristics of the dragon. How fast can it move compared to a human? Illustrate the stages in its life cycle;
- Ask the students to imagine a myth associated with their dragon;
- Encourage some students to apply their dragon drawings into other art concepts, such as heraldry. Can they design a family coat of arms that contains a dragon?;
- Time permitting, go beyond where we reached in this unit.

Lee Yuen Lew is a teacher and researcher at Ross Middle School, East Hampton, New York. E-mail: llew@ ross.org John W. McLure is Associate Professor of Curriculum and Instruction, University of Iowa, Iowa City. E-mail: John-mclure@uiowa.edu

REFERENCES

Ashton-Warner, S. (1963). *Teacher*. New York: Simon and Schuster.

Ball, S. (1985). *Porguacan*, a mini-flip-flop book. West Germany. Ars Edition.

Bates, Roy. (2002). *Chinese dragons*. New York: Oxford National Academy Press.

Brooks, J., & Brooks, M. G. (1993). *The case for constructivist classrooms*. Alexandria, VA: Association for Supervision and Curriculum Development.

Elkins, J. (1999). *The domain of images*. Ithaca, NY: Cornell University Press.

Fisher, J. (1988). Jean Fisher on Joan Fontcuberta and Pere Formiguera. *Art Forum International*, 27(2), 141–142.

International Reading Association. (1996). *Standards for the English Language Arts*. Urbana, IL.: National Council.

Kilpatrick, W. H. (1918). The project method. *Teacher's College Record, XIX*(4), 319–335.

Lew, L. Y. (2001). *Development of constructivist behaviors among four new science teachers prepared at The University of Iowa*. Unpublished doctoral dissertation in science education, The University of Iowa.

MacCurdy, E. (Trans.). (1955). *The notebooks of Leonardo da Vinci*. New York: George Braziller.

MENC. (1994). *National standards for arts education*. Reston, VA: Music Educators National Conference (MENC).

National Center for History in the Schools. (1994). *National standards for world history*. Los Angeles, CA: University of California.

Perrone, V. (1994). How to engage students in learning. *Educational Leadership, 51*(5), 11–13.

Phillips, D. C. (1995). The good, the bad, and the ugly: The many faces of constructivism. *Educational Researcher, 24*(7), 5–12.

Stevens, K. G. (2001). *Chinese mythological gods*. Oxford University Press.

Walker, D. (2003). *Fundamentals of curriculum*. Mahwah, NJ: Lawrence Erlbaum Associates, Inc.

Yager, R. E. (1991). The constructivist learning model: Towards real reform in science education. *The Science Teacher, 58*(6), 52–57.

Yager, R. E. (2000). The constructivist learning model. *The Science Teacher, 67*(1), 44–45.

Zubov, V. P. (1968). *Leonardo da Vinci*, translated from the Russian by David H. Krass. Cambridge, MA: Harvard University Press.

SAMPLE INTERNET RESOURCES USED BY THE STUDENTS

http://www.crystalinks.com/chinadragons.html

http://sorrel.humboldt.edu/~geog309i/ideas/dragons

http://lair2000.net/Dragon_Lair

http://www.mythicalrealm.com/images2/chindragon

http://home.earthlink.net/~jonesofnh/evildragons.html

http://www.dartmouth.edu/artsci/ethics-inst/images/Brain.jpg

http://www.ywconnection.com/pageRfirebreathingdragoncake.html

Name:_____

SAMPLE ARTMAKING WORKSHEET

Theme: Creating your own Imaginary Creature (The dragon as an inspiration)

Medium: Drawing, Mixed Media (cardboard box, fabric, wiggly eyes, sequins, feathers, etc.)

Objectives: Students will learn to create their own imagined creatures that represent themselves by studying the signs of the Chinese Zodiac. Students learn about the culture that inspired the imagined creature, the dragon. Students learn to think imaginatively and engage with possibilities in multiple contexts.

Integration Area(s): Arts, Cultures, Language Arts, and Science
We learned that the Chinese calendar has a 12-year cycle based on lunar calendar.[53] Each of the 12 signs of the zodiac is represented by an animal, each of which represents different personality traits and characteristics. Your task is to create an imagined creature that represents your personality traits and characteristics based on the year you were born, as inspired by the Chinese dragon.

Characteristics of Chinese Dragon: Chinese dragons are prestigious among the zodiac animals as symbols of good luck and good fortune. The dragon is also unique among the signs; in that, it is a visual composite of parts of nine animals: the horns of a deer; the head of a camel; the eyes of a devil; the neck of a snake; the abdomen of a large cockle; the scales of a carp; the claws of an eagle; the paws of a tiger; and the ears of an ox. The dragon is also a symbol of magical power. It can fly or swim. It can even bring rain. It has been at least 6000 years since it was first conceived.

Figure 3. The dragon is illustrated by Elizabeth Uitvlug.

[53] The 12 animal signs are the rat, ox, tiger, rabbit, dragon, snake, horse, sheep, monkey, rooster, dog, and pig.

Culture and Arts Integration

1. What's your DOB? _____ 11 / 11 / 1996 _____

2. What's your animal sign based on the 12 signs of the Chinese zodiac system?[54]
   _____ Rat _____

3. What does the zodiac sign say about you (characteristics/qualities)?
   _____ generous , creative , charming , imaginitive _____
   _____
   _____

4. How does it represent you personally (accept/reject/adopt)?
   _____ Accept _____
   _____
   _____

5. List things you learned or already knew about Chinese Dragons, their history, their types and their role in Chinese culture:
   _____
   _____
   _____

6. One thing that you learned about your traits/characteristics from the 12 signs of the Zodiac system was:
   _____ I am quick-tempered _____
   _____
   _____

7. One way that Chinese dragons influenced your design was:
   _____
   _____
   _____

8. One new thing that you learned about yourself while making the artwork was:
   _____
   _____
   _____

[54] The Chinese Zodiac is calculated according to Chinese lunar calendar. You will need a copy of Chinese Zodiac to find your zodiac animal sign. See website: http://www.living-chinese-symbols.com/12-chinese-zodiac-sign.html

SAMPLE ARTMAKING WORKSHEET

Theme: What is your favorite animal (e.g., dog, cat, bird, exotic animal, small mammal, etc.)?

Medium/Strategy: Drawing from observation: Perceptual Drawing

Objectives: Students will choose their favorite animal to draw and learn about the interaction of species through food chains and webs (ecosystem)[55].

Artist Integration: George Rodrigue, Key Artwork: Blue Dog Painting.

Language Arts Integration: Students will write a sentence including three adjectives that describe you and your favorite animal. For example, my favorite animal is a dog, because it is loyal, fun and trustworthy just like me.

Life Science Integration: Students will learn about Food Chain and Food Web[56] about their favorite animal. Students will then draw their favorite animal in the center of the box, and identify its food chain. For example, sea turtles' enemy is a shark and they will eat small fish and insects. Food chains follow a single path as Humans → Sharks → Sea Turtles → Fish/Shrimp → Sea Weeds.

Quaternary Consumers (Eat tertiary consumers)	
Tertiary Consumers (Eat secondary consumers)	
Secondary Consumers (Carnivores: meat-eaters) and Omnivores: animals that eat both animals and plants)	
Primary Consumers (Herbivores: plant-eaters)	
Primary Producers (Autotrophs: organisms that make their own food from sunlight and/or chemical energy from deep sea vents)	

---

[55] Defined as a biological community of interacting organisms and their physical environment—Wikipedia.
[56] Food webs show how plants and animals are interconnected by different paths. For more information about food webs and food chains in ecosystem structure and function, please see tutorVista.com at http://www.tutorvista.com/content/biology/biology-iv/ecosystem/food-web.php

Visual Art Integration: After students draw their favorite animal, students will be introduced with the Blue Dog paintings of George Rodrigue. They will create an image of their favorite animal in a fantasy environment, using colored oil pastels as a means to express feelings.

CURRICULAR ISSUES: THE VISUAL ARTS AND STUDENTS WITH DISABILITIES

R. GLORIA PAPPALARDO

REACHING OUT TO REACH WITHIN

As we enter the 21st century in education, we must be concerned with a quality visual arts education for all students. Every elementary and secondary school should provide a sequential visual arts curriculum that integrates the study of art production/creative expression, aesthetics, art criticism/analysis, and art history/culture. Because the visual arts have always been considered a universal language and a discipline that reaches out to all students, we must plan and create a visual arts curriculum that includes the student with a disability. The study of the visual arts develops the intellect and increases visual sensitivity, therefore enabling the student to identify and solve problems more effectively through manipulation of materials and/or verbal discussion. More and more schools are mainstreaming and/or including students with disabilities in a general education classroom. One will find less self-contained "art classes" for students with disabilities. These students have become a part of the general educational program requiring the provision of the least restrictive situation and more involvement with general education students and society.

As this has occurred, little has been done by school districts to prepare the visual arts specialist with knowledge or assistance as to means for working with students with disabilities or addressing curriculum or units of study for these students. Visual arts specialists struggle with how to reach the student with disabilities, often watering down the unit of study or lesson and/or lowering standards for them. This chapter is designed to provide some information for visual arts specialists who work with mainstreamed and/or included students with disabilities. It is the point of view of this writer that with a basic understanding of the students with disabilities, the art specialist can adapt the regular visual arts curriculum, allowing students an opportunity to enjoy positive visual arts experiences and an opportunity to express themselves verbally and visually. Thus, the visual arts will become a natural part of their learning process and of great value to students' abilities to create their own images and forms, and to make aesthetic inquiries, as well as informed judgments and understanding of art history and culture based on knowledge and experience.

"How do you treat a person with a disability?" "How do you plan a visual arts program for a person with a disability?" By far, the most important thing to keep in mind is that the student is an *individual* first—an individual who just happens to have a disability; you are dealing with a *person*, not a *label*. Many barriers faced by students with disabilities are attitudinal. For instance, many people see them as "different" and treat them as such. The teacher should treat them as any other students deemed more "able," concentrating on their *strengths* rather than their weaknesses; be *positive* and *honest*.

You will discover that these students have much in common with you and all other people, and then you will cease to be uncomfortable. The population of people with disabilities includes individuals who have speech, hearing, or vision impairment, or physical, emotional, mental, or learning disablilities. Within each category of disability, the range and variation of personalities and traits are as extensive as with all people. In general, people with physical and mental disabilities have the same desires to succeed as anyone. The visual arts give them the opportunity to express themselves both verbally and visually, developing self-worth and self-esteem.

The more you know about specific disabilities, the more comfortable and natural you will feel around people with disabilities. You will enjoy knowing them as individuals and be able to concentrate on what they *can do*, rather than on what they cannot do. Units of study will stress their level of learning and/or style of learning including the same concepts and objectives. The visual arts curriculum will be adjusted to meet the needs of the student with disabilities, but not "watered down."

How Do You Treat the Special Person?

In understanding students with special needs you must realize that some students have multiple disabilities. For example, a person with mental retardation may also be visually impaired; a student who is deaf might have an emotional disability; a person with a physical disability may also have a learning disability. While the disabilities have been categorized under specific headings, you may need to incorporate several of the teaching methods or areas discussed, based on the students' needs. Keep in mind that some individuals may be on medication that may make them appear lethargic.

Try to reduce competition by avoiding comparisons between individuals' work with the group, especially in a mainstreamed or included situation. Vary your method of presentation, allowing for alternatives that may work better. Include demonstrations, role-playing and movement, visual reinforcement, oral as well as written instructions, and tactile (feeling or touching) experiences.

The enthusiasm you generate will be contagious. Patience—Patience—Patience! Verbal and nonverbal praise encourages continued interest and motivation. Don't be afraid to reward appropriately. Your positive attitude will be recognized by students with special needs and by nondisabled students and will create a positive environment for all. Seek assistance from the child study team. They are great support professionals. Check students' Individualized Education Program (IEP) and participate in writing it.

When teaching art lessons, it is often better to *show* the students than to *tell* them how to do something. When speaking, seek eye contact and call students by name. Allow students to work independently. If an aide or another student helps the student with disabilities, don't let them rob the student with a disability of his or her opportunity to create.

If someone has a seizure (convulsion) in the art room, follow these rules:

- Clear away any objects on which the student might be injured if he or she falls or flails.
- Do not try to restrain his or her movements.
- Do not force anything between the student's teeth. He or she will *not* swallow the tongue.
- The convulsion should be over in less than 2 minutes. If he or she does not appear to be coherent after the seizure, send for help. Alert medical personnel of the situation.
- Be calm—do not overreact and upset others.

GENERAL INFORMATION

Learning Disabilities (Neurologically Impaired, Perceptually Impaired)

A student with a learning disability generally has average or above average intelligence and can learn at the same time rate as his or her age peers. Unfortunately, the method of learning is somewhat different. He or she has trouble with one or more of the following skills: listening, thinking, speaking, reading, writing, spelling, arithmetic, fine and gross motor coordination. This student needs success, large and small! All visual arts activities should be organized from simple to complex in order for the student to experience some positive success. Give directions one step at a time, using varied methods: verbal, visual, and kinetic. If teaching art history/culture, doing aesthetic scanning or critical analysis allow the student time to think and respond verbally. Make positive comments and ask leading questions.

The student with a learning disability may

- Become frustrated easily. Reduce this by limiting directions, background noise, visual confusion, space.
- Be clumsy and awkward or have trouble making his or her hands do what the eye sees.
- Exhibit disruptive behaviors such as restlessness, short attention span, or a hostile attitude. Do not assume that the student is not enjoying the activity. It could be that he or she is afraid of sounding foolish, of making a mistake, or of becoming frustrated.

When working with a student with a learning disability

- Give extra motivation and lots of praise. Establish and maintain routines (time patterns).
- Give directions in single units. For instance, instead of saying "Take out your art journal, and using pencil and white paper, copy the vocabulary words in column one," *instead say*, "Take out your art journal (pause) now open to a clean page and take your pencil (pause), find the vocabulary column one (demonstrate). Now copy the words into your journal." This rule applies to older students as well as to younger ones.
- Provide secluded and/or quiet areas for students with distraction problems.
- Offer a choice of media for exploring techniques and skills. Allow for individual needs.
- Be aware of low frustration levels. Help the student address the problem and deal with it.
- Be positive and praise when necessary, always considering a student's self-esteem.
- A buddy student or an aide will be helpful in keeping the student on target. Be sure the person only helps the student with a disability with *understanding* the problem but *does not do the task for him or her*.

Orthopedic Disabilities (Orthopedically Handicapped)

An individual with an orthopedic disability has a condition that prevents or slows down the ability to move. People with physical disabilities can be recognized as those requiring, for example, wheelchairs, crutches, braces. Some may have involuntary musculature movements or sensory loss. Individuals with physical disabilities may or may not have mental retardation. Do not assume that someone with limited motor and communication abilities has mental retardation. Some common types of physical disabilities are cerebral palsy, muscular dystrophy, spina bifida, and others that may have occurred due to an injury.

The person with a physical disability may

- Have a poor hand grasp.
- Have jerky or shaky motions and uneven body movements.
- Have a startled reaction when approached or suddenly touched.
- Often trip or fall if ambulatory.
- Have difficulty in imitating motor movements.
- May move slowly due to crutches, braces, or a wheelchair.
- May not have all his or her limbs.

When working with individuals with physical disabilities:

- Be sure materials are easily accessible and use adaptive devices, if needed, to increase independence. Use appropriate materials (i.e., wider pencils for handgrip, squeeze scissors, and open-mouth containers for paint or paste for uneven body movements).

- Many people with physical disabilities can move around independently and maneuver their own wheelchairs. Some may require assistance with ramps, doors, etc. However, *ask if they need help before you give it.* Remember that they are dealing with their disability and don't rob them of their independence.
- Ensure that facilities are accessible, appropriate, and safe. Remove unnecessary obstructions when experiences are designed to motivate physical exercise.
- When planning, ensure that there are opportunities for personal expression and self-worth.
- Allow twice as much time for movement.

Emotional Disabilities and Behavioral Disorders

The person with an emotional disability may exhibit one or more of the following characteristics, which adversely affect educational performance:

- An inability to learn that cannot be explained by intellectual, sensory, or health factors.
- Inappropriate behaviors or feelings such as being easily frightened or having irrational fears.
- Inability to build interpersonal relationships with peers or teachers.
- A pervasive mood of unhappiness or depression or rapid mood change.
- Physical symptoms of behavior associated with personal or school problems (i.e., hostile attitude, destructive behavior, impulsive behavior).
- Avoidance of direct eye contact.
- Responsiveness to directions by squirming or being hostile.
- Hyperactivity or withdrawal.
- Need for an unusual amount of prodding to complete a given task.

When working with the individual with emotional disabilities, check with support personnel. Follow the general guidelines for a consistent, well-coordinated planned behavior program. Observe the following general guidelines:

- Have lessons as structured as possible but flexible with individual expression. Give the student a small amount to do at one time with praise at each step to encourage completion.
- Provide the student with activities in which he or she is able to expand energy positively, foster confidence through quickly achieved success, and build on it.
- Have a minimum of supplies within reach, particularly if they can be spilled or broken. Give verbal and nonverbal recognition for efforts.
- Give the student extra attention if he or she responds to it, but do not force attention on the student if he or she withdraws. Reward positive behavior with concrete or nonverbal (i.e., wink, smile) expression.
- Encourage group discussions on personal expression through arts to help the student learn to express his or her emotions (anger, joy, sadness) in appropriate ways.
- Identify each person's individual space where the student feels safe and cared about.
- Establish procedures, rules, and expectations and follow them consistently. Be prepared by planning alternatives and appropriate steps for discipline. If a student's behavior becomes too disruptive, send for help. *Do not* leave the group.
- Look at the student when you ask short questions. Listen attentively.

Behavioral Disorders (Socially Maladjusted)

The personal with a behavioral disorder has a consistent inability to conform to the standards for behavior set by the school. Characteristics include

- Difficulty with interpersonal relationships with peers or adults.
- Inappropriate behaviors such as fighting and loud talking.
- Rebelliousness to authority figures.
- Difficulty accepting authority figures.
- Behaviors that reflect hostility and possible destructiveness.
- Extreme difficulty in following socially expected behaviors and school rules.

When working with the student who has a behavioral disorder, be sure to check with support personnel and/or administration in order to be as consistent as possible and maintain realistic expectations.

- Be as positive as possible.
- Give the student activities that are within his or her capabilities.
- Provide positive reinforcement when appropriate and possible.
- Follow exactly the disciplinary plan specified by support personnel and administration.
- Establish procedures, rules, and expectations.

Visually Impaired (Visually Handicapped)

Only 10% of the legally blind population in America has complete loss of sight or only light perception. The other 90%, termed "visually impaired" by the American Foundation for the Blind, has varying amounts of residual vision.

A person who is legally blind is simply someone who cannot see as well as his sighted counterpart; intelligence level is not affected by being blind.

The problem of *mobility* is probably the biggest concern for individuals who are blind. Never go up to a person who is blind and grab an arm to lead him or her around. Rather, when working with a person who is visually impaired, ask if he or she would like to take your arm and be guided. Keep the following things in mind when guiding a person who is blind:

- Stand next to, and a little ahead of the person. Bend your arm at the elbow, allowing his or her hand to be placed on your forearm.
- Walk normally, but perhaps a little slower.
- Give verbal cues along the way to orient the person to his or her surroundings.
- Give advance warnings of potential obstacles (a flag pole, an exhibit case, any protruding object, etc.).

In a world of accurate visual perception, it is crucial that the blind person be provided with (a) the opportunity to handle the object he or she is learning about, and (b) a guide who is able to give a detailed accurate description of the visual world around him or her.

For the sight-impaired, *touching is seeing*. If you are demonstrating a craft, allow the person to place his or her hands on yours as you demonstrate the activity. If the lesson was planned as a cut-and-paste activity, have the person feel the form and tear it. Place your hands over his or hers as you explain the activity.

When working with individuals with visual impairment, remember to

- Identify yourself and let them know that you are talking to them.
- Tell them if you are leaving before you walk away.
- Avoid using gestures and other visual communication that would not be available to them.
- Speak in a normal voice. Blind people are not deaf.
- Talk as you would normally. Do not be embarrassed to use words like "see" and "look."
- Remember, touching is not the only way a person who is blind can learn. If you provide a detailed verbal description of an object or of what you are doing, it can be visualized in the mind's eye. Include a description of everything: texture, weight, scent, size, volume, and even color. Try to keep the description concrete and related to familiar things. For example, rather than saying a tepee is a conical shape, compare the shape to an upside down ice cream cone. Some people who are blind have trouble with spatial relationships. Rather than describing the size of something in feet and inches, say, "It is the size of your index finger," or "if two people as tall as you stood on your shoulders, that's how tall it would be."
- Sometimes it is helpful to give directional assistance by using the clock face method. "Your crayon is at 1:00, your paintbrush is at 7:00."

Hearing Impairments (Auditorily Handicapped)

The term *deaf* refers to a profound degree of hearing loss that prevents understanding speech through the ear. "Hearing impaired people" or "people with a hearing loss" are expressions used to indicate any degree of hearing loss, mild or profound.

A hearing impairment affects the individual's ability to learn auditorily, but he or she has some degree of usable hearing that can be improved via a hearing aid.

If the person lost his or her hearing before the age of three, he or she will have been deprived of the opportunity to establish a solid language base. As a result, a deaf person will usually be lacking in language skills, including reading and writing skills. However, it is very important to remember that inadequate language skills are not indicative of low intelligence.

When communicating with a deaf person, you must remember that he or she receives messages visually, and may depend upon lipreading or manual communication. If you are talking to someone whom you do know to be a lipreader, keep the following things in mind:

- Avoid changing your message suddenly, as in saying, "By the way, does anyone know what time it is?"
- Try to be in good lighting when talking to the person so he or she may be able to see your lips.
- Never look away or cover your mouth while you are speaking.
- Do not try to overcompensate for the person's hearing loss by shouting. Often that will result in a distortion of sound.
- Use simple, basic language, speaking clearly and at an even pace.

Many persons who are deaf are trained in the use of total communication, where a combination of sign language and finger spelling as speech is used. To many deaf people, English is a second language; they talk and think in pictures. The passive voice and slang have no place in their language. Therefore, even if you are being translated by an interpreter, keep your verbal usage simple and basic, avoiding abstractions.

Give verbal and nonverbal instructions and praise through expressions and gestures when working with people who are deaf and hearing impaired.

When working with people who are deaf and hearing impaired:

- Emphasize nonverbal communication as much as you can. Use facial expressions and gestures to help communicate your thought. Demonstrate or act out the message you have for the person! Draw a picture.
- Carry a pad and pencil around with you to jot down key words or phrases or for any questions the person may have.
- Deaf individuals have varying abilities of spoken language skills. Listen carefully and try to understand what they are saying. If you cannot understand, do not get upset or make the person feel bad. Simply ask him or her to repeat what he or she said slowly, first; then have him or her write the question down or to act it out. Remember to repeat the question/statement to the whole class.
- Try to avoid coming up suddenly from behind deaf people. Since they cannot hear you coming, they can be startled, and can have balance or coordination problems. Be careful of quick movements that would make them dizzy.
- It is very important to let them physically manipulate objects around them.
- Remember that deaf people cannot look at an object and hear an explanation for it at the same time. The instructor needs to explain what it is they will be seeing. *Give them ample time to view and handle it*; then repeat any important instructions or explanations, slowly and clearly.
- Explore using all the senses to encourage students to communicate in nonverbal ways to more effectively express themselves.

Mental Retardation (Mentally Retarded)

A person with mental retardation is characterized by a below-average intelligence functioning and by defects in adaptive behavior. Often he or she will behave like a person much younger in age. Often he or she will progress through normal development stages but at a slower rate than other youngsters.

Degrees of mental retardation are described as:

- Mild—Individuals with mild mental retardation have the ability to learn basic academic skills and are commonly referred to as EMR (Educable Mentally Retarded). Ninety percent of individuals with mental retardation fall into this category. They can be taught the same projects as general education students but will probably take longer to finish them.
- Moderate—Individuals with moderate mental retardation are able to learn some academic, communication, social, and occupational skills. This category is commonly referred to as TMR (Trainable Mentally Retarded). They often need a greater level of direct supervision. For example, in this group are individuals with Down syndrome or with hydrocephalic, and microcephalic conditions.
- Severe/Profound—Individuals with severe/profound mental retardation are characterized by more limited abilities. They require continual close supervision. Usually they can learn basic self-care skills such as washing, toileting, and feeding, and most can benefit from some training in language development and physical mobility. Persons with profound retardation are sometimes completely dependent on others for all their needs. Only 5% of individuals with mental retardation fall into this category.

Depending on the degree of the disability, a person with mental retardation might

- Exhibit poor motor and hand/eye coordination.
- Have a short attention span.
- Have a low frustration level.
- Learn best by imitation (a proper role model is important).
- Have poor abstract reasoning ability.
- Have difficulty seeing fine detail.
- Have little self-direction in choosing activities.
- Exhibit inappropriate behavior.
- Be overly affectionate, wanting to cling or hug.

When working with people with mental retardation, establish simple, consistent procedures and rules.

- Keep directions simple; break the task into progressive steps; demonstrate each task.
- Provide frequent motivation and praise.
- Be patient and allow extra time to observe and think.
- Use repetition in directions and actions. Identify all materials verbally.
- Deal in concrete ideas and terms with which they will be familiar; don't assume ability to generalize or associate from past experience.
- Use multisensory approaches to motivate.
- Allow and encourage the students to do their own work; step-by-step procedures will ensure this.
- Take a student's hands and guide him or her through the motions if the process is too difficult.
- Avoid paying attention to distractions.
- Remember that these individuals *are* capable of *learning* and are able to appreciate new experiences.
- Encourage cooperation and assistance among students.
- Plan lessons within their ability range, not chronological age.
- Encourage discussing art forms, how they were created, how they make you feel.
- Remember, they will give honest, simple answers—accept them with praise.

Preschool Delays (Preschool Handicapped)

Children between ages 3 and 5 may have developmental delays or disabilities of any type or types (language difficulties, speech problems, motor problems, etc.). These children require specialized intensive programming in a small class that may be located in the school district or elsewhere. Often occupational therapy, physical therapy, and/or speech therapy is necessary.

Generally, these children have limited academic mainstreaming or included opportunities because of their age, but they can participate in school events like assemblies and programs. When working with these children, keep in mind

- Their young chronological age.
- The possible disparity of developmental levels with age.
- The need for clear, simple, verbal messages.
- The need to be a part of the school community.

- The ability to profit and learn from being with nondisabled children.
- The possible inability to identify themselves, their address, and their telephone number.
- The need to use materials (such as paint, clay, paper, wood) in order to develop skills and use of appropriate tools or equipment.
- The need to use the visual arts as a means of expression both verbal and visual.

Communication Disabilities (Communication Handicapped)

A student with a communication disability has difficulty receiving and expressing information particularly when language is involved. Despite average intelligence, the student often appears not to understand clearly what is being said. Thus, responses are not accurate nor completely related to questions posed or information presented.

This student requires limited directions, clear and concise statements, and clarification of concepts. Use of visual clues is often helpful.

When working with a student with a communication disability:

- Be sure that he or she understands what is to be done.
- Use short, simple verbal directions and provide written ones as well.
- Clarify understandings, especially word meanings.
- Keep auditory and visual distractions to a minimum.
- Try to establish eye contact when conversing with him or her.
- Use visual images to explain a procedure.
- Use visual images created by the student to express his or her feelings or ideas.

CONCLUSIONS

The classifications used in this chapter are current terminology. The terms in parentheses are unique to the State of New Jersey. Other states may have different categories to identify students with disabilities. Recognizing the disability will enable the reader to concur with the terms unique to that respective state or part of the country. The New Jersey State Department of Education is preparing a curriculum framework for grades K through 12 at the present time. The framework will include an addendum including the basic visual arts curriculum for *all* students, including those with disabilities.

Students with disabilities will develop intellectual and visual sensitivity through visual arts experiences. The visual arts will enable them to identify and solve problems more effectively and allow them to make more positive contributions to society. Allowing these students to not only create art, but to talk about art, to view art, and to study art history and cultures will open broader horizons for them and allow them to more effectively be included in the school and community they live in.

In planning units of study in the visual arts for students with disabilities, the art specialist must keep in mind the student whose disability they are working with. Visual arts lessons must be planned carefully, allowing for the disability, but the curriculum must be developed to address a most positive, involved environment that will include *all* students. It is through patience and careful planning and working with other professionals, both art and special educators, that this is achieved.

The writer is aware that a small self-contained classroom of students with like disabilities might be easier to plan for and teach visual arts in, but this is not always the least restrictive environment. Educational settings should be offered that include the opportunity to have social experiences and interaction with all students. In some cases this is the *best* environment but not the *least restrictive*.

Each student will have an IEP (Individualized Education Program) developed by the Child Study Team, a plan that includes parental involvement. The art specialist should be aware of the IEP in order to better address the needs of the student. If possible, the art specialist should participate in meetings in which the team plans the IEPs for those students they are working with. Many school districts mainstream and/or include special population students in the general education visual arts classes. It is our obligation as art specialists to plan lessons carefully to include these students, so they may meet success and develop further feelings of self-worth as well as have better opportunities to function in society and enjoy a finer quality of life. If an aide isn't available for visual art classes, perhaps a student in an upper class can come in to assist while gaining credit for community or school service.

The mainstreamed situation and/or inclusion does work in the visual arts classroom. Be Patient—Be Calm—Be Positive!

RESOURCES

Isaacs, Illene. Executive Director, Very Special Arts New Jersey, editing and personal conversations. 703 Jersey Avenue, New Brunswick, NY 08901.

"Kids on the Block." Series of programs of puppet performances that teach audiences what handicaps are all about. Handicapped puppets used to explain their feelings and needs. Audience participation and handicapped awareness. Heidi Goldstein, 201-379-1700.

Miele, N., Director of Special Services and Pappalardo, R. G. Supervisor of Visual Arts. Co-authors, *Students with disabilities: Understanding their needs. A guide for teachers— "Reaching out to reach within."* Randolph Township Schools, 6 Emery Avenue, Randolph, NJ 07869. 201-662-8899.

New Jersey Administrative Code Title 6 Education, Chapter 28 Special Education, Division of Curriculum and Instruction, 1994-1999 N.J.A.C.6:28.

Nutley, J. Very Special Arts of Indiana. Indianapolis, IN 46240.

Schectman, A. E., Certified Art and Special Education Educator, personal conversations.

Schectman, A. E. (1995, September). *Insights: Art in special education: Educating the handicapped through art in special education* (6th rev. ed.). Cherry Hill, NJ: Art Educators of New Jersey. A guide for teachers of art and special education including lesson plans designed to meet needs of students with disabilities.

Very Special Arts Educational Programs, John F. Kennedy Center, Washington, DC 20566. This group provides current media, publications, and resources on the disabled.

Name: _____

IN-CLASS DISCUSSION QUESTIONS

Pappalardo's Curricular Issues: The Visual Arts and Students with Disabilities

1. What are different types of special needs (disabilities)?

2. What is the role of visual arts for students with disabilities? What is the author trying to advocate through visual arts curriculum?

3. How do you treat students with special needs?

4. What are some strategies for teaching students with special needs?

5. What is an IEP? Why does a student need one?

ASSESSING STUDENTS WITH SPECIAL NEEDS IN ART

Assessment is an integral part of the art curriculum, as it drives the purposes and goals of art learning. When it comes to assessing students with special needs in artmaking, it can be challenging.[55] Art educators often face these questions: *How many disabilities does a student have? Which disabilities are involved? How severe (or moderate or mild) is each disability? How does each disability affect student's learning, use of the senses, and ability to make art?* The need for assessment in art increases in difficulty for special needs students because art is often used for therapeutic purposes or a psychological outlet to exorcise our emotional excess. So what should be assessed? Art activities should be carefully designed to develop student's cognitive and affective understanding, using visual repertoires for expression of ideas or storytelling. Different tactile materials and artmaking techniques should be adapted and designed carefully to help students participate in art projects that enable them to identify and solve problems, along with broaden their horizons when participating in school and in society.

The assessment criteria thus should focus on a student's learning process and development of the level on cognitive and affective domains. Assessment should identify the levels of capacity, emphasize process over product, strengths over weaknesses, and avoid personal judgments or labeling, along with indicating skills required to perform tasks that demonstrate their level of knowledge, skill, and understanding. The assessment should avoid watering down the content or oversimplified concept than those of their peers.

Additionally, by providing further comments and suggestions for future improvements and by working with other teachers and school personnel, assessment in art can be a powerful tool that helps students with disabilities access grade-level content and ensures appropriate accommodations are provided along with their IEPs goals.[56]

Example of Assessment Chart in an Art Experience Activity

Criteria/Scale	Baseline	Developing	Adequate	Self-Governing	High Functioning
Cognitive Domain					
Affective Domain					
Skill Acquisition					
Expressivity					
Self-Motivation					
Behavior					
Further comments and suggestions for future improvements					

---

[55] Gerber, Beverly Levett, and Doris M. Guay. *Reaching and Teaching Students with Special Needs through Art.* Reston, Va.: National Art Education Association, 2006.

[56] IEP stands for individualized education program (plan). The *individualized* part of IEP means that the plan has to be tailored specifically to meet a student's special needs—not to be based on the needs of the teacher, the school, or the district. Goals, modifications, accommodations, personnel, and placement should all be selected, enforced, and maintained with the particular needs of a student in mind.

General Information to be Considered

The term "disability" is defined by the Americans with Disabilities Act (ADA) of 1990 as "a physical or mental impairment that substantially limits one or more major life activities."[57] A student can be identified with multiple disabilities, and these multiple disabilities are often unrecognized or developed at a later time and are not all the same across the individuals (age, gender, race, etc.) Thus, these students with more than one impairment or disability can be difficult to accommodate (i.e., a severe Down's syndrome student may have a cognitive impairment along with a verbal or language difficulty–communication disability). Art can be a great way for students with disabilities to be able to communicate their thoughts and personal views of the world. Art teachers should focus on the student's abilities rather than on what they cannot do, as more students with disabilities enter the classroom and are often taught in the general education classroom. Therefore, art teachers will need to know how to effectively teach all students regardless of a disability. When working with special needs students in an inclusive setting, art teachers need to learn how to provide a positive and safe environment for all students, using visual arts to support students with disabilities to recognize and develop problem-solving skills by using visual repertoires or manipulating materials.

Pappalardo[58] suggests:

- Do not water-down the content
- Concentrate on strengths not weaknesses
- Allow more time on task and be flexible
- Treat students as individuals (with as much respect as you would with any others)
- Lessons need to be carefully planned and adapted to meet the needs and interests of the students
- Provide concrete and visual example for intended lesson outcome
- Repeat instructions with step-by-step written instructions on the board
- Provide step-by-step demo to show students rather than tell them how to do something
- Provide one-on-one assistance or in small group work with peer assistance
- Keep positive attitudes: Be Patient – Be Calm – Be Positive – Be Sensitive!!!

[57] https://adata.org/faq/what-definition-disability-under-ada
[58] Pappalardo, Gloria. "Curricular Issues: The Visual Arts and Students with Disabilities." *In Introduction to Integrating Music, Art, and Theatre in Elementary Education*, edited by Allison Metz, Beth Gibbs and Hsiao-ping Chen, pp. 101–110. Dubuque, IA: Kendall Hunt Publishing, 2011.

How to Involve and Adapt Visual Arts for Students with Disabilities[59]

Types of Disabilities	Characteristics	Adaptations/Strategies in Classroom
Learning Disabilities (LD)	A student with a learning disability generally has average or above-average intelligence and is struggling with academic performance and difficulties in listening, thinking, speaking, reading, writing, spelling, arithmetic, and/or motor coordination	• Art activities should take a "hands-on" approach to instruction. Project themes should focus on interests and desires of the students (i.e., what is your favorite animal? What's your favorite place to go to?) • Directions begin from simple to complex tasks, by giving one direction at a time, and various methods. • Group work is something that will help the students work on their relationship and teamwork skills. • Teach students strengths, and progress will be made with the student. • Suggested mediums: drawing, painting, photography.
Physical Disabilities (Orthopedic Impairments)	A student with a physical disability has limitations on mobility or is impaired physically in a wheelchair, crutches, or braces, including those with neuromotor impairments, cerebral palsy and neuromuscular disabilities.	• Art activities or projects should focus on the skills/abilities of each individual student, not all students with physical disabilities present in the same way. • Techniques and strategies must be customized, use special (adapted) tools such as squeeze scissors and adapted or larger brushes for grasping or manipulating art materials. • Make sure materials and the art-room space are easily accessible for wheelchairs, wide doorways, and tables with adjustable height. • If recourses allowed, use computer-assisted technologies or adapted digital tools (Kidpix or other apps) for drawing or painting purposes. • Work with OT (occupational therapists), PT (physical therapists), SLP (speech language pathologists) to learn about strengths and weaknesses of the student. • Suggested medium: digital painting.

(Continued)

[59] Pappalardo, Gloria. "Curricular Issues: The Visual Arts and Students with Disabilities." In *Introduction to Integrating Music, Art, and Theatre in Elementary Education*, edited by Allison Metz, Beth Gibbs and Hsiao-ping Chen, pp. 101–110. Dubuque, IA: Kendall Hunt Publishing, 2011.

Emotional Impairments (EI)	A student with an emotional disability is identified as having an inability to learn that which cannot be explained by intellectual, sensory, or health factors and typically has a general pervasive mood of unhappiness or depression or fears associated with personal or school problems, along with an inability to build or maintain satisfactory interpersonal relationships with peers or teachers.	• Art activities or projects should focus on fine motor skills, focusing on individual expression, drawing upon personal stories, talking about all of the feelings. (anger/sadness/stress) or coping mechanism. • Establish procedures and firm rules, keep positive teaching attitude, take the time to know the student, look at students when asking them a question, and have structured but flexible lessons depending on their moods. • Create a student self-check list and structured schedule for the student to keep at their side. • Suggested medium: painting, drawing, photography, etc.
Behavioral Disorders	A student with a behavioral disorder has a difficult time following the standard behaviors set by the school, including those of attention-deficient/hyperactivity disorder (AD/HD), oppositional defiant disorder (ODD). Shown difficulties in creating interpersonal relationships, accepting authority figures, and some may experience impulsive behaviors, due to feelings or emotions sudden change.	• Art activities or projects should be short and highly motivating, focusing on developing interpersonal skills and management of behaviors. • Give extra attention/time to meet the standard rules set by the schooling system. • Be consistent as possible! Establish rules and guidelines; use reward for positive praise/feedback. • Designate a corner chair for calm time; prepare squeeze ball or bouncing ball ready for an emotional outbreak or stress release. • Suggested medium: painting, drawing, photography
Cognitive Impairments (CI)	A student with a cognitive impaired has a below-average intelligence level or adaptive behaviors, included those of Down's syndrome, characterized as mild, moderate, and severe depending on the disability and the student's ability to learn that he or she may have poor judgment and reasoning skills, attention to irrelevant details, short-term memory problems.	• Art activities or projects should focus on concrete not abstract thinking, to develop social skills, and increasing self-awareness, self-esteem, and self-control. • Keep projects short, provide step-by-step directions, with visual aids and prompts, repeat directions as many as possible, with choices making opportunities • Suggested: painting, drawing, photography

(Continued)

Hearing Impairments	A student with a hearing impairment may experience different levels of hearing loss or impairment.	• Art activities or projects should emphasize nonverbal communication as much as possible; speak clearly when giving instruction. Remember, a deaf student talks and thinks in pictures. • Use nonverbal instructions or talk slowly with clear communication. Make sure to be in good lighting in order for the person to read your lips; use basic language and never look away when you're speaking. • Suggested: drawing, painting, sculpting
Visual Impairments	A student with a visual impaired is defined as either having little or highly impaired vision or being "legally blind" with no vision.	• Art activities or projects should focus on sense of touch while creating art instead of using sight. • Mobility is the biggest concern, touching is seeing, give verbal clues on their surroundings, allow the blind student to physically touch what is being learned about when possible. If not possible, assign the student an aide to give a detailed visual description of what is going on. • Suggested: clay sculpting
Preschool Delays or Early Childhood Developmental Delay (ECDD)	A student in preschool delayed at age (3–5 years) has not learned or developed at a much slower rate developmentally particularly with problems in language, speech, or motor-related issues.	• Art activities or projects should focus on both visual and verbal expression. • Suggested: painting, drawing.
Speech or Language Impairments	A student with a speech or language impairment, identified with a communication disorder, has problems with speech, language, voice, fluency, or social communication. Such as autism spectrum disorders (autism), Asperger, and Angelman syndrome.	• Art activities or projects should focus on expressions of self or storytelling, using visual images and prompted with written and clear and concise statements, making sure the student understands what is needed. • Suggested: painting, drawing, photography.

Name: _____

SAMPLE WORKSHEET FOR PLANNING AN ART ACTIVITY EXPERIENCE FOR SPECIAL NEEDS STUDENTS

- This project is specifically designed to be adapted for students with a _____ disability (maybe multiple).

  Definition of the disability:

- Identify characteristics of the disability, including student behaviors and skills, strengths and weaknesses associated with this disability:

- Identify your goals for the project to be complete by these students.

- Core concepts to be learned:

- Skills acquirement (e.g., motor skills, abstract thinking, counting, painting, drawing):

- Materials needed (e.g., jumbo markers, crayons, color pencils, glitter, feathers, construction paper, recycled materials, white glue, scissors):

- List instructions and strategies based on individual interest, abilities, and different learning styles for completing the project (activities/steps, such as may require one-on-one or a small group setting):

- List adaptations and modifications to be incorporated into the project for inclusion of students with the disability.

- Design a worksheet for developing student's conceptual understanding on art activity based on your list of adaptations and theme or concept listed above. A visual example of intended project outcome should be provided.

Name: _____

SAMPLE ARTMAKING WORKSHEET[60]

Study the American and Japanese Zen Gardens

A field trip to Frederik Meijer Gardens and Sculpture Park is encouraged if you are resided in Grand Rapids, Michigan. If a field trip to a garden is not accessible, a set of photos of different types of gardens, American and Japanese, can be Googled and printed out for students as an alternative.

Adaptations

This project is intended to be taught in an inclusive art classroom for older elementary students and students with cognitive impairments (mild or moderate). Students with verbal difficulties (communication impairments) might be assisted with one-on-one help in explaining the worksheet and the sketch of garden design.

Brainstorming Activity: Developing Student's Concept of a Garden

Ask students to write down their responses (before visiting the gardens)

- What is a garden[61]? How is a garden defined?

- Where does the garden end and nature begin?

- Who creates a garden? (Who decides?)

- Why do we have a garden? (For what purpose?)

- What can be in a garden? (Criteria and elements of garden.)

---

[60] This hands-on Japanese Zen-inspired garden project is developed based on a visit to the Japanese garden (just open in 2016) in Frederik Meijer Gardens and Sculpture Park in Grand Rapids, Michigan. Frederik Meijer gardens are most famous for providing botanical and sculptural arts gardens that engage visitors with sensory and cultural experiences with the nature.

[61] A garden is defined as "a planned space, usually outdoors, set aside for the display, cultivation, and enjoyment of plants and other forms of nature" (https://en.wikipedia.org/wiki/Garden).

Name: _____

IN-CLASS DISCUSSIONS: DEVELOPING STUDENT'S HIGHER-ORDER THINKING THROUGH IDENTIFICATION, COMPARISON, AND CONTRAST

Ask students to write down the elements in the gardens they see that are different and similar between American and Japanese and how the two different cultures affect the meaning, purpose, and function of a garden design. Use the Venn diagram to tell how the gardens are alike and how they are different.

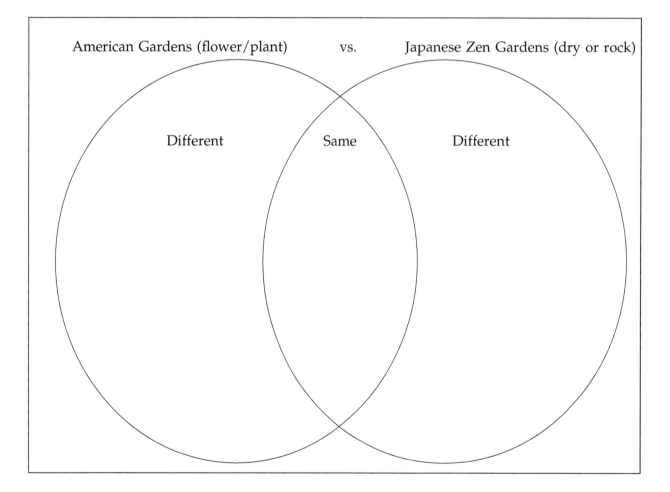

American Gardens (flower/plant)   vs.   Japanese Zen Gardens (dry or rock)

Different   Same   Different

Write down your definition of a Japanese garden and an American garden

A Japanese garden is

_____.

An American garden is

_____.

Name: _____

HANDS-ON ART ACTIVITY: CREATE A ZEN-INSPIRED MINIATURE GARDEN (AFTER THE VISIT OF THE GARDENS)

Materials needed: artificial flowers/plants, coffee powder for dirt, beans, colored pebbles, rocks, moss, sand, seashells for decoration, play-dough for plant bases, 10 x 10-inch sort colored construction papers for base color, one 10 x 10-inch cardboard for the garden base, four precut sticks of 3/8 thick x 10-inch-long balsawood for boarders) and others seen applicable. Recommended natural and edible food for decoration (i.e., cereal, jelly beans, fish crackers can be adapted).

Rationale for your garden design/type:
Purpose of the garden:
Criteria/or influences of your design from Japanese cultures or gardens:
What should be in the garden? List elements for your garden (i.e., bridges, islands, stones, shrubs, sculptures, flowers, ponds, shorelines, sand, pebbles, trees, waterfalls, streams, paths, architecture):
Name of your garden:
Design of your Zen-inspired garden:

REFERENCES

Ballengee-Morris, Christine, and Patricia Stuhr. "Multicultural Art and Visual Cultural Education in a Changing World." *The Journal of Art Education* 54, no. 4 (2001): 6–13.

———. "Multicultural Art and Visual Cultural Education in a Changing World." *Art Education* 54, no. 4 (2001): 6–13.

Barrett, Terry. "Interpreting Visual Culture." *Journal of Art Education* 56, no. 2 (2003): 6–12.

Beane, James. *Curriculum Integration: Designing the Core of Democratic Education.* New York: Teachers College: Columbia University, 1997.

Boriss-Krimsky, Carolyn. "Stages of Artistic Development." In *The Creativity Handbook: A Visual Arts Guide for Parents and Teachers,* 22–63. Springfield: Charles C Thomas Publisher, 1999.

Carpenter, Stephen. "An Editorial: The Return of Visual Culture (Why Not?)." *Journal of Art Education* 58, no. 6 (2005): 4–5.

Clark, Gilbert , Michael Day, and Dwaine Greer. "Discipline-Based Art Education: Becoming Students of Art." *Journal of Aesthetic Education* 21, no. 2, Special Issues: Discipline-Based Art Education (1987): 129–93.

Crawford, Donald. "Aesthetics in Discipline-Based Art Educationdonald W. Crawford." *Journal of Aesthetic Education* 21, no. 2, Special Issue: Discipline-Based Art Education (1987): 227–39.

Daniel, Vasta, and Patricia Stuhr. "Suggestions for Integrating the Arts into Curriculum." *Journal of Art Education* 59, no. 1 (2006): 6–11.

Ducumn, P. "Visual Culture: Developments, Definitions, and Directions for Art Education." *Studies in Art Education* 42, no. 2 (2001): 101–12.

Duke, Leilani. "The Getty Center for Education in the Arts and Discipline-Based Art Education." *Journal of Art Education* 41, no. 2 (1988): 7–12.

Duncum, Paul. "Clarifying Visual Culture Art Education." *The Journal of Art education* 55, no. 3 (2002).

———. "Instructional Resources: Visual Culture in the Classroom." *Journal of Art Education* 56, no. 2 (2003): 25–32.

———. "Visual Culture: Developments, Definitions, and Directions for Art Education." *Studies in Art Education* 42, no. 2 (2001): 101–12.

———. "What Elementary Generalist Teachers Need to Know to Teach Art Well." *Journal of Art Education* 52, no. 6 (1999): 33–37.

Efland, Arthur. "Antecedents of Discipline-Based Art Education." *Journal of Aesthetic Education* 21, no. 2, Special Issue: Discipline-Based ArtEducation (1987): 57–94.

———. *Art and Cognition: Integrting the Visual Arts in the Curriculum.* New York: Teachers College: Columbia University, 2002.

Eisner, Elliot. *The Arts and Creation of Mind.* New Haven: Yale University Press, 2002.

Freedman, Kerry. "The Importance of Student Artistic Production to Teaching Visual Culture." *Journal of Art Education* 56, no. 2 (2003): 38–43.

———. *Teaching Visual Culture.* New York: Teachers College Press, 2003.

———. *Teaching Visual Culture: Curriculum, Aesthetics and the Social Life of Art.* New York; Reston, VA: Teachers College Press; National Art Education Association, 2003.

Gerber, Beverly Levett, and Doris M. Guay. *Reaching and Teaching Students with Special Needs through Art.* Reston, VA.: National Art Education Association, 2006.

Giroux, Henry. *Disturbing Pleasures: Learning Popular Culture.* New York: Routledge, 1994.

Hamblen, Karen. "What Does Dbae Teach?" *Journal of Art Education* 41, no. 2 (1988): 23–24, 33–35.

Keifer-Boyd, Karen, Patricia Amburgy, and Wanda Knight. "Three Approches to Teaching Visual Culture in K-12 School Contexts." *Journal of Art Education* 56, no. 2 (2003): 44–51.

Kleinbauer, Eugene "Art History in Discipline-Based Art Education." *Journal of Aesthetic Education* 21, no. 2, Special Issue: Discipline-Based Art Education (1987): 205–15.

Lowenfeld, Viktor. *Viktor Lowenfeld Speaks on Art and Creativity*. [Washington: National Art Education Association, 1968.

Lowenfeld, Viktor, and W. Lambert Brittain. *Creative and Mental Growth*. 4th ed. New York,: Macmillan, 1964.

McFee, June King, and Rogena M. Degge. *Art, Culture, and Environment : A Catalyst for Teaching*. Dubuque, Iowa: Kendall/Hunt Pub. Co., 1980.

Neperud, Ronald. *Context, Content, and Community in Art Education: Beyond Postmodernism*. New York: Teachers College Press, 1995.

Parsons, Michael. "The Arts and Other Subjects." *Studies in Art Education* 41, no. 3 (2000): 195–96.

———. "Integrated Curriculum and Our Paradigm of Cognition in the Arts." *Studies in Art Education* 39, no. 2 (1998): 103–16.

———. "The Role of the Visual Arts in the Growth of Mind." *Studies in Art Education* 46, no. 4 (2005): 369–77.

Pappalardo, Gloria. "Curricular Issues: The Visual Arts and Students with Disabilities." In *Introduction to Integrating Music, Art, and Theatre in Elementary Education*, edited by Allison Metz, Beth Gibbs and Hsiao-ping Chen, pp. 101–110. Dubuque, IA: Kendall Hunt Publishing, 2011.

Risatti, Howard "Art Criticism in Discipline-Based Art Education." *Journal of Aesthetic Education* 21, no. 2, Special Issue: Discipline-Based Art Education (1987): 217–25.

Sandell, Renee. "Form+Theme+Context: Balancing Considerations for Meaningful Art Learning." *Journal of Art Education* 59, no. 1 (2006): 33–37.

———. "Using Form+Theme+Context (Ftc) for Rebalancing 21st-Century Art Education." *Studies in Art Education* 50, no. 3 (2009): 287–99.

Smith, Ralph. "The Changing Image of Art Education: Theoretical Antecedents of Discipline-Based Art Education." *Journal of Aesthetic Education* 21, no. 2, Special Issues: Discipline-Based Art Education (1987): 3–34.

Smith-Shank, Deborah. "Lewis Hine and His Photo Stories: Visual Culture and Social Reform." *Journal of Art Education* 56, no. 2 (2003): 33–37.

Spratt, Frederick "Art Production in Discipline-Based Art Education." *Journal of Aesthetic Education* 21, no. 2, Special Issues: Discipline-Based Art Edcuation (1987): 197–204.

Stewart, Marilyn, and Sydney Walker. *Rethinking Curriculum in Art*, Art Education in Practice Series. Worcester, Mass.: Davis Publications, 2005.

Tavin, K. "Hanuntological Shifts: Fear and Loathing of Popular (Visual) Culture." *Studies in Art Education* 46, no. 2 (2005): 101–17.

———. "Wrestling with Angels, Searching for Ghosts: Toward a Critical Pedagogy of Visual Culture." *Studies in Art Education* 44, no. 3 (2003): 197–213.

Taylor, Pamela, and Christine Ballengee-Morris. "Using Visual Culture to Put a Contemporary "Fizz" On the Study of Pop Art." *Journal of Art Education* 56, no. 2 (2003): 20–24.

Toku, Masami. "What Is Manga?: The Influence of Pop Culture in Adolescent Art." *The Journal of Art Education* 54, no. 2 (2001): 10–17.

Villeneuve, Pat. "Why Not Visual Culture?" *Journal of Art Education* 56, no. 2 (2003): 4–5.

Walker, Sydney. "Artmaking, Subjectivity, and Signification." *Studies in Art Education* 51, no. 1 (2009): 78–91.

———. "How Shall We Teach? Rethinking Artmaking Instruction." *Teaching Artist Journal* 4, no. 3 (2006): 190–97.

———. *Teaching Meaning in Artmaking*, Art Education in Practice Series. Worcester, Mass.: Davis Publications, 2001.

———. "Understnding the Artmaking Process: Reflective Practice." *Journal of Art Education* 57, no. 3 (2004): 5–12.

———. "What More Can You Ask? Armaking and Inquiry." *Journal of Art Education* 56, no. 5 (2003): 6–13.

————. "Working in the Black Box: Meaning-Making and Artmaking." *Journal of Art Education* 50, no. 4 (1997): 23–31.

Wilson, Brent. "Child Art after Modernism: Visual Culture and New Narratives." In *Handbook of Research and Policy in Art Education* edited by Elliot Eisner and Michael Day, 247–76. NJ: Mahwah: Lawrence Erlbaum., 2004.

————. "Figure Structure, Figure Action, and Framing in the Drawings of American and Egyptian Children." *Studies in Art Education* 21, no. 1 (1979): 36–43.

————. "Of Diagrams and Rhizomes: Visual Culture, Contemporary Art, and the Impossibility of Mapping the Content of Art Education." *Studies of Art Education* 3, no. 44 (2003): 214–29.

————. "The Superherroes of J.C. Holz:Plus and Outline of a Theory of Child Art." *Journal of Art Education* 27, no. 8 (1974): 2–9.

Wilson, Brent, and Masami Toku. "Boys' Love, *Yaoi,* and Art Education: Issues of Power and Pedagogy." In *Semiotics and Art/Visual Culture,* edited by Deborah Smith-Shank. Reston, Virginia: The National Art Education Association, 2003.

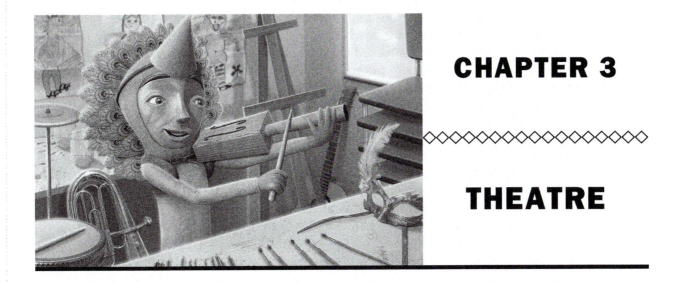

CHAPTER 3

✕✕✕✕✕✕✕✕✕✕✕✕✕✕✕✕

THEATRE

DRAMATIC ACTIVITIES FOR CURRICULAR GOALS

Many preservice teachers assume that in order to use drama in their classrooms they themselves must be able to "act." However, all the acting skills they need are already employed during their "act" of teaching. When teachers create a new lesson plan, stand up in front of their students, vocally command young people's attention, and model their expectations, they are communicating via the tools of the actor.

There are three main tools, or instruments, of the actor that all teachers employ in the classroom: mind (creativity), body, and voice.[1] Mind, body, and voice give actors the means to communicate ideas and emotions with an audience. Teachers use the same tools to transfer information to their students and need to pay attention to the messages their tools are broadcasting. Effective teaching includes paying attention to your own:

BODY posture, gesture, and stance—An instructor who has weight equally distributed between both feet, open hand gestures, and is standing up straight commands attention and gives an appearance of easy confidence. A slouching teacher who has crossed arms over their chest and crossed feet looks guarded, insecure, and off putting. If you would like to invite participation in your classroom, begin by showing them that you are a secure teacher willing and capable to support their educational endeavors.

VOCAL volume, tones, and pace—Aim to speak to the back of your classroom when you are presenting ideas to students in order to make sure you are loud enough for everyone to hear. At the very least, take a few deep, slow breaths before you begin teaching in order to warm up your breath, which supports your voice. Also, think about how vocal inflection affects your command of a group. For instance, in conversation, many people have the habit of raising inflection at the end of a sentence, making their words appear like a question instead of a statement.

MIND (creativity)—Artists of all kinds are inspired by other art, and the same is true for the art of teaching. Use lesson plans and ideas from other educators as starting points to motivate yourself to create variations for your specific population. Remember a lesson from high school that you loved? Think about WHY you loved the lesson so much and adapt it for your younger students. Just about any lesson can be modified for a different group and most younger students just need a little more guiding (or "scaffolding" of directions and activities, which is described later in this chapter) to successfully complete lessons geared toward older ager groups.

[1] Barton, Robert. *Acting: Onstage and Off.* (Fort Worth, TX: Harcourt Brace College Publishers, 1992).

Students can enhance their own acting tools through dramatic activities. By integrating dramatic activities into their lesson planning, teachers can start conscientiously enhancing their students' acting skills and exploring standardized curriculum in a memorable and fun way.

What makes an interactive classroom pursuit a dramatic activity? A classroom game is a dramatic activity if (1) the activity primarily utilizes the tools of the actor and (2) the activity is interactive. As previously discussed, actors utilize three main tools for their craft: imagination, body, and voice. If students utilize any combination of the actor's three tools, then classroom games become dramatic activities. Interaction during a dramatic activity can occur in many ways, whether it is based in cooperation or competitive play. Keeping in mind that theatre is a collaborative art form, cooperative games augment a group's sense of community when they assemble and work together to achieve their objective. If teachers want to "raise the stakes" for students, competitively played dramatic activities can serve as an appropriate vehicle, where one person or a small team "wins" the game, although lower risk cooperative games more aptly fulfill students' sense of self-worth without having to worry about "losing."

While you read about dramatic activities, consider how theatre games for the classroom are a viable technique for:

- Enhancing teamwork in a classroom community.
- Utilizing communication skills.
- Kinesthetically engaging learners.
- Making curriculum memorable and fun.

Five Examples of Dramatic Activities for the Classroom

Educational drama experts cite many reasons why dramatic activities enhance the learning process. In *Creative Drama for the Classroom*, Ruth Beall Heinig writes about the "psychological security" drama activities provide for generating good feelings in a relaxed atmosphere. When Viola Spolin, a leader in the improvised theatre movement of the twentieth century, writes about why teachers should bring theatre games into the classroom, she assures teachers that "Playing theatre games with your students will bring refreshment, vitality, and more."[2] Spolin notes that theatre games improve students' verbal and non-verbal communication skills, increase energy, develop awareness, deepen critical thinking processes, and team work.

Dramatic activities can function as engagement activities at the beginning of a lesson, the building blocks of longer lessons, and reflective practice at the end of a class. Variations of dramatic activities allow teachers to mold theatre games to individual needs of their students and demands of their curriculum. Once a teacher understands the mechanics and purpose of a certain dramatic activity, the teacher should feel comfortable creating adaptations of the activity for different purposes.

The following five examples of popular theatre games are uniformly formatted so that teachers new to dramatic activities can comfortably lead these activities, no matter their prior acting experience. Elements are further explained and give teachers questions to think about when they are cataloguing their own games and dramatic activities. Every attempt has been made to cite similar games in other published sources, although many of these games flourish because of the oral tradition.

- Title of activity: *Name of game.*
- Objective: *What is the overall goal for playing this game, specifically in a curricular context?*

---

[2] *Theatre Games for the Classroom, 2*

- Target age: *Pick ONE age. Many games can be modified to play with people of all ages, but more specifically, gearing toward developmental stage leads to clearer instructions. Planning for ONE grade level or ONE age group on paper will clarify the planning process on paper.*

- Number of participants: *Number of players.*

- Room arrangement: *Think about space requirements for the dramatic activity. Will tables, chairs, or desks need to be moved out of the way? Can students stay behind their desks or will everyone need to sit in a circle?*

- Materials (if any): *Prepare yourself with papers, pens, notecards, etc.*

- Similar to: *Many dramatic activities are passed on through an oral tradition. Similar games can be found in other published sources, which the author of this book has provided for additional reference points. Games should be considered intellectual property and subject to plagiarism. When possible, teachers should acknowledge published sources (title and author) in their lesson plans. Always name the source of the material, just as you would with any published material.*

- Description of the activity: *Clearly written "rules" for the game.*

- Curricular connection: *Subject areas where dramatic activities connect to standard curriculum, such as language arts, social studies, science, etc.*

- Variations: *Any single dramatic activity can be played in multiple ways, depending on objectives and age of players. Variations allow the teacher to consider adaptions for given needs and prepare for the "next level."*

The following dramatic activities are examples of well-known, well-received dramatic activities for classroom use. There are numerous other examples that could have been included in this text and these are intended to serve as a sample. For more ideas about activities to include in your classroom, please refer to the "Theatre Works Cited and Resources" section.

1. **Title of activity: NAME DANCE GAME**

   Objective: *To learn names of people in the classroom.*

   Target age: *All ages.*

   Number of participants: *Between 8 and 25.*

   Room arrangement: *Clear space for everyone to stand and move in a circle.*

   Materials (if any): *None.*

   Similar to: *"Dance of Names," 101 Dance Games for Children, Paul Rooyackers.*

   Description of the activity: *Everyone stands in a circle. Participants think of a simple movement that goes along with the syllables of their name. When it is a player's turn, he or she steps forward, says his or her name, and makes a movement to go along with each syllable. The rest of the group repeats the player's name and movements. The next participant steps forward, says their name with a movement for each syllable, which everyone then rehearses together. As a group, everyone then does the first person's name and movement, followed by the second person's name and movement. The third person shares their name and movement. After everyone rehearses the third person's name and movement, the group simultaneously does the first person's, then the second person's, then the third person's, etc. until everyone has been added on in the Name Dance Game.*

   Curricular connection: This is a wonderful, kinesthetic game to play at the beginning of the year when people are learning each other's names; however, it can also be applied to learning names of historical figures in social studies, new vocabulary words in language arts, or remembering sequencing of steps for math problems.

Variations: Players move around the room repeating one person's name and movement, then the teacher signals (i.e., hand clap) when it is time for the next person to share their name and movement.

Players can also work in pairs, repeating each other's names and movements. The teacher signals with a sound or flickers the lights when it is time for everyone to switch partners.

2. **Title of activity: "THIS IS A..."**

Objective: To creatively show original ways to use objects.

Target age: Any age.

Number of participants: No more than 15.

Room arrangement: Students in a circle will help everyone see other players, or one player at a time can be called up to the front of the room.

Materials (if any): Any objects can be used, although less familiar objects will prompt more ingenuity.

Similar to: "Object Transformation,"*The Creative Classroom*, Lenore Blank Kelner.

Description of the activity: When the player receives the object, they must stand up, talk about an imagined use for the object, and show (pantomime if necessary) the imaginary use for the object. The object is passed around until everyone has a turn.

Curricular connection: This activity is a great warm up for creative writing in a language arts lesson. For older students, using an unidentified artifact or tool can engage a group at the start of a unit in social studies or science.

Variations: In order to develop critical thinking and improvisation, students ask the object holder questions about the item's imaginary use.

For an added challenge, students silently pantomime the object's function and the audience writes down a name for the object. This variation can be done in complete silence until the end, when students verbally share their ideas.

3. **Title of activity: WOO-HOO!, OH!, ZIP!**

Objective: To physically and verbally concentrate on a fast paced task.

Target age: Third grade and up.

Number of participants: Up to 30.

Room arrangement: Clear space for everyone to stand and move in a circle.

Materials (if any): None.

Description of the activity: Participants stand in a circle. Game begins with just the "Woo-hoo!" step (see directions later). The teacher then adds the "Oh!" phase before finally including the "Zip!" part.

Woo-hoo!—Players use their entire bodies as they say "Woo-hoo!" to pass the sound and movement to the player next to them, who sends it on to the next person, so on and so forth, as the "Woo-hoo!" goes around the circle in the same direction.

Oh!—Players say "Oh!" and hold up both hands in front of their chests in a stop motion. The player who just received the "Oh!" must reverse the direction of the "Woo-hoo!" *The ONLY response to an "Oh!" is a "Woo-hoo!" (In other words, a player cannot "Oh!" an "Oh!")

Zip!—When a player receives a "Woo-hoo!" they can send a "Zip!" to any other player in the circle by making eye contact with their intended target, stepping and clapping toward that player, as they say "Zip!" The person who has received the "Zip!" now has to send a "Woo-hoo!" to one of the players on either side of them (the "Zip!" receiver can send the "Woo-hoo!" either way around the circle. *The ONLY response to a "Zip!" is a "Woo-hoo!" (In other words, a player cannot "Oh!" a "Zip!")

Curricular connection: This dramatic activity is best used as an energizing game or reward activity which encourages students to focus their energy. The game can also be used to activate concepts that you are learning about, such as reasons for electricity flow and redirection in a science lesson.

Variations: Game can be played competitively, with people getting "out" for not correctly following directions, or cooperatively, where all players stay in throughout the game.

4. **Title of activity: CHIEF**

   Objective: To critically observe and follow actions.

   Target age: First grade and up.

   Number of participants: 8–30.

   Room arrangement: Students will need to sit or stand in a circle.

   Materials (if any): None.

   Similar to: "Who Started the Motion?" *Theater Games for the Classroom*, Viola Spolin.

   Description of the activity: One player, the "guesser," leaves the room in order for a leader to be selected. Once everyone knows who the leader is, the leader will start a repetitive movement (i.e., shaking head, shrugging shoulders, and alternately pointing fingers). The guesser returns to the room and stands in the middle of the circle. The leader will switch up the motions every 10–15 seconds. The guesser has three chances to figure out who is leading. The rest of the group will try to challenge the guesser by not looking directly at the leader, or engaging in any other behavior that will "tip off" the guesser. Once the guesser has correctly deduced who the leader is, or they have used up their three guesses, then another guesser and another leader are chosen.

   Curricular connection: Students of all ages enjoy this challenging and fun dramatic activity, which often gets used as a focusing warm-up, or an active reward for the end of a good school day. However, with thoughtful questioning, a teacher can also use this game as an engaging metaphor to talk about moments when masses of people worked together to change history, such as the Civil Rights movement, allied countries ending World War II, and the Boston tea party.

   Variations: Teachers can make this game more challenging by limiting the movements the leader can make, such as playing a round when the leader only uses facial expressions, or only uses one arm.

5. **Title of activity: SHOWING A STORY**

   Objective: To help students understand and describe elements of literature.

   Target age: Second grade.

   Number of participants: Groups of three to six people.

   Room arrangement: Open floor space with a distinct stage area.

   Materials (if any): Index cards with predetermined characters (who), settings (where/when), conflicts, and objective/plot (what).

   Source: Malinda Petersen, Grand Valley State University Instructor, MAT 300.

Description of the activity: A brief discussion with students begins with the teachers asking students to think about a story they like. The students are also prompted with questions: Who was your favorite character? Was there a challenging part of the story? What happened at the beginning, middle, and end?

Students are put into small groups. Each group is given a card for a who, what, where, and conflict. The students must create a story using the words from each card, rehearse, and show the teacher the story using their bodies and voices.

Curricular connection: Common Core State Standards for English Language Arts. http://michigan.gov/documents/mde/CCSSI_ELA20Standards_395332_7.pdf?201310291131547

"Ask and answer such questions as who, what, where, when, why, and how to demonstrate understanding of key details in a text. Describe how characters in a story respond to major events and challenges. Describe the overall structure of a story, including describing how the beginning introduces the story and the ending concludes the action. Use information gained from the illustrations and words in a print or digital text to demonstrate understanding of its characters, setting, or plot."

Variations: This could be used for middle and/or high school students with the grade level terms for the elements of literature. Actual props and set pieces could be introduced. The first time though only gibberish language can be spoken. The cards could have words referring to a social studies or science lesson for cross-curriculum. A writing exercise could follow with each student expanding on the story.

DRAMATIC ACTIVITY LITMUS TEST

*Is your activity **actually** a dramatic activity?*

Sensory work	Narrative pantomime	Simple improvisation
Guided imagery	Pantomimed improvisation	Situation role-playing
Movement work	Sound and verbal work	Teacher-in-role

*To test it, **does it fit into one of the categories below?***

If the answer is YES, the next question is:

Are participants using their minds, bodies, and voices?

If you can answer YES to both of the above questions, then YES, you have a dramatic activity!
If you are answering NO, how can you adapt the activity or tweak it to fit?
Use your MIND and CREATE.   **PLAY!**

["Dramatic Activity Litmus Test" handout created by Malinda Petersen, January 2014, Grand Valley State University, MAT 300 instructor]

[handwritten: how to tell if an activity is dramatic]

Top Sixteen "Tips" for Leading Dramatic Activities in the Classroom

Please keep in mind that the following tips are based on the assumption that teachers lead interactive, cooperative classroom activities in order for students to feel successful as they reach curricular benchmarks while having fun in the process:

1. STAGGER (SCAFFOLD) DIRECTIONS: Provide directions in steps so that the group feels successful. If you are teaching a complicated game, then let your class just try the first level of the game before you bring in the next level.

2. MAKE SURE YOU HAVE EVERYONE'S ATTENTION WHEN YOU GIVE DIRECTIONS: Think about classroom formation when you give directions and make sure everyone can see/hear you while you tell them what to do. Children, especially, will lose focus if you try to regain their attention *after* they spread around your space, so make sure you tell them everything they need to know before they move around room, or make sure you have everyone's attention before you give additional directions.

3. IF YOUR CLASS IS IN A CIRCLE, GIVE DIRECTIONS FROM THE CIRCLE OR KEEP TURNING AROUND IN CENTER: Lots of dramatic activities require a circle formation. Either provide directions as you stand as part of the circle or if you have to stand in the center, make sure you keep turning around so you don't have your back to any of your students while you provide directions.

4. MODEL PARTICIPATION: SHOW your students what you want them to do by providing an active example.

5. KNOW WHEN TO START GAME: Sometimes participants want to keep asking questions when it is easier to show them how to play a game instead of explaining it. Start the game and only stop if there's confusion.

6. SIDECOACH: Share encouraging comments as students are playing that will keep them focused on the objective of the activity. Think about your role as a coach for the game instead of a silent supervisor. (See Spolin, *Theatre Games for the Classroom*.)

7. OFFER *SPECIFIC* POSITIVE FEEDBACK: Let your students know what their exact strengths are so they can capitalize on them. It feels very satisfying when someone tells you "Good job," but how do you know what was "good?" Instead of saying "Great work," provide a *specific* example of what students are doing well: "It was great how focused everyone stayed on the activity."

8. USE POSITIVE PHRASING INSTEAD OF NEGATIVE DIRECTIONS: For example, reminding your students, "This is a silent activity," instead of saying "Don't talk" creates a nurturing classroom environment. This is a teaching skill that may take some work for new teachers, but the benefits are worth it!

9. MOVE AROUND ROOM TO MONITOR AND ENCOURAGE SMALL GROUP WORK: In order to ensure everyone is on task and to keep confusion to a minimum, move around your classroom so you are readily at hand for students who need your help.

10. PLAY ALONG WHEN YOU CAN: If your goal is to create a cooperative, classroom community where participants can take risks, then showing your students that you are willing to play along and take your own risks will establish a safe space faster.

11. PLAY LONG ENOUGH FOR PARTICIPANTS TO FEEL SUCCESSFUL AND HAVE FUN: Fight the urge to move on to another activity as soon as everyone is playing along with the non-competitive game. Allow your students the chance to enjoy playing before they have to move on to something else.

12. KNOW WHEN YOU ARE PERFORMING "SCENES" AND WHEN YOU ARE PERFORMING "SKITS": "Skits" are great in recreational settings (summer camps, after-school programs, etc.) because there is a connotation of fun and silliness. "Scenes" are more appropriate for school since there is an implication that the performance can either be fun or serious. This

difference in terminology can result in more thoughtful classroom work and less pressure to produce something funny.

13. MAKE SURE CHEWING GUM IS OUT OF YOUR MOUTH BEFORE YOU START TEACHING: Nothing more distracting than watching your teachers chew their gum instead of listening to their directions! Gum also interferes with enunciation and tone.

14. ONLY ASK QUESTIONS YOU *REALLY* WANT TO KNOW THE ANSWER TO: Teachers ask questions like "Does that sound fun?" and "Do you want to find out what happens next?" only imagining a positive response. However, what happens if the group says "NO!?" Whether it really sounds fun to the students, or if they truly want to find out what happens next, these types of questions tend to be redundant and disingenuous so why bother asking when the students have no choice where the lesson is going next?

15. CONSIDER GENDER NEUTRAL ADDRESSES TO THE GROUP INSTEAD OF CONSISTENTLY EMPLOYING SEXIST PHRASES SUCH AS OVERUSING "YOU GUYS. . . . :" Although a phrase like "You guys" is generally accepted as a phrase that addresses a mixed gender group, it is still a male-based, colloquial phrase. Instead of constantly referring to a group as "You guys," try using more inclusive phrases such as "everyone," or "my friends."

16. MAKE SURE STUDENTS GET ON THEIR FEET AND REHEARSE BEFORE SHARING ANY SORT OF PERFORMANCE WITH OTHERS:Talking about a plan or performance is very different from rehearsing ideas in action. Encourage groups to begin rehearsing scenes and performance moments as quickly as they can in order to adequately prepare before sharing with any sort of audience.

Connecting "Games" to State and National Standards

As the principal approaches your classroom, she hears children laughing and clapping amid moments of abrupt silence. When she peeps into your classroom through the window, the principal sees desks pushed to the sides of the room, children scattered around in frozen poses attentively watching you for the next command. You, the classroom teacher, give a direction and the room explodes in movement as smiling children travel around the room as if they were frogs. Your principal thinks to herself, "Frogs? What does playing like frogs have to do with school?" What will you say to her when she asks you the same question?

There are two ways to connect dramatic activities and theater arts with state and national standards: incidentally and directly. Incidentally, the skills enhanced during the process of using theater crossover with general skill sets that will help young people become valued members of our democratic society. Students gain advantageous attributes include heightened imagination, engagement, and participation. Merryl Goldberg, author of *Arts Integration: Teaching Subject Matter through the Arts in Multicultural Settings* writes that the arts are "fundamental tools for educating students in character, developing reflective minds, and encouraging healthy bodies" (p. 216). Directly, classroom teachers are responsible for meeting benchmarks outlined in national and state standards. State standards can be found on the Arts Education Partnership website, under the "State Policy Database," at www.aeparts.org/database.

Historical Influence: Viola Spolin

Starting in the 1930s, Viola Spolin (b. November 7, 1906–d. November 22, 1994) impacted methods of dramatic improvisation for generations to come, in theatrical rehearsal spaces, improvisational performance venues, and elementary school classrooms. Spolin admitted that her greatest inspiration began in 1924 as she embarked on a career as a settlement worker in Neva Boyd's Group Work School in Chicago. Boyd's innovative teaching methods with immigrant and inner-city children sparked Spolin's ideas about structuring games in order to enhance interpersonal relationships. After working as a drama supervisor for Chicago's Works Progress

Administration's Recreational Project from 1939 to 1941, Spolin's development of games for creative expression led to her formation of the Young Actor's Company in Hollywood in 1946, where children learned acting methods via theatre games. After moving back to Chicago in 1960, Spolin began working extensively with her son, the late playwright and teacher Paul Sills, and leading theatre games workshops for Second City, television shows, and movies. Spolin's *Theatre Game File* (1975), and her books *Improvisation for the Theatre (1963), Theatre Games for Rehearsal* (1985), and *Theatre Games for the Classroom, Grades 1–3* and *Grades 4–6*, as well as a 1979 Honorary Doctorate degree from Eastern Michigan University, established Spolin as a pioneer in the field of educational drama and improvisational theatre. Spolin's techniques, "based on the assumption that players will make educational, psychological, and social gains as they participate in theatre games," highlighted leader as coach, side coaching, focus, and problem-based evaluation.[3] Viola Spolin's influence on theatre games for educational purposes continues today to ripple through classroom and rehearsal spaces as teachers and directors use her published resources to help their students explore their world through dramatic activities.

Spolin References: Rosenberg, Helene S. and Patricia Pinciotti. *Creative Drama and Imagination: Transforming Ideas into Action* (New York, Holt, Rhinehart, and Winston, 1987) 38–42.

Spolin, Viola. *Theatre Games for the Classroom: A Teacher's Handbook.* (Evanston, IL: Northwestern University Press, 1986).

"The Spolin Center." http://www.spolin.com/violabio.html

[3] Rosenberg, 40–42.

Name: _Jamie Gibbons_

DISCUSSION QUESTIONS

Please type your responses to each question on a separate hard copy, OR legibly hand write directly on this page (use back of sheet as needed) and hand in. Each response needs to be at least 3 sentences long (3 sentences = minimum requirement for a paragraph)

1. What memorable game experiences do you have from your own time in school? Were the games used as simple rewards for you and your classmates, or were they tied to subject areas, such as language arts or history? First, talk about whether these games were "dramatic activities" and if not, why; second, discuss how you could alter the games from your childhood to fit curricular objectives.

   In school games were most often used as study tools. We participated in Jeopardy games before big tests in almost all of my high school classes. Our games were dramatic because they included sound and verbal work when we shared answers and we had to stand and give loud answers if we wanted to get the points before the other team.

2. Find a "dramatic activity" through researching websites and books (try to pick a game or activity that you could use for a dramatic activity teaching assignment, or in a future classroom). Create THREE variations of the dramatic activity, and explain how you would use the activity for different ages/developmental stages, and/or standard curricular areas, such as science, social studies, health, or other content areas.

3. Out of the list of "Top Sixteen Tips," talk about one tip that you *already* use in your teaching and one tip that is *new* to you. Cite an example from your personal experience, as a student or as a teacher, that illustrates one, or both, of the tips.

LESSON STRUCTURES: STORY DRAMA AND ROLE DRAMA

This section will share ways in which you can employ longer lesson structures, namely story drama and role drama, in your classroom to:

- Create memorable and engaging lesson plans using a series of dramatic activities.
- Help students understand real world situations within the safety of dramatic play.
- Activate learning within the language arts curriculum.
- Dynamically explore curricular topics outside of language arts curriculum.
- Recognize the importance of scaffolding in character work.
- Understand the distinction between *role drama* and the *Mantle of the Expert* technique.

Story Drama

Once teachers have established a cooperative, supportive learning community in their classrooms through short, low-risk dramatic activities, they can begin to build longer lessons using stories as source material for story drama. Story drama is one of the many ways teachers can start to integrate more extensive drama lessons into their curriculum. Story drama brings stories to life when students actively engage in the narrative, or when dramatic activities are used to explore related themes. Carefully planned drama lessons, followed by thoughtful reflection, will nurture inventive, cooperative, and dynamic student contributions in the classroom.

Planning drama lessons: Planning drama lessons requires the same basic steps necessary for planning any classroom lesson, except that variations of dramatic activities focus the participants on the story, or topic, at hand.[4] Preparing drama lessons includes the following five steps:

1. Engagement activities: Also known as "warm-ups" or "starter activities," preliminary activities will engage students intellectually, physically, and/or verbally with the topic of the lesson.[5] Paired with a "hook" (such as a preset prop in plain view that will be used later in the lesson) engagement activities effectively draw students into a given lesson.
2. Share story or discuss topic: In a language arts lesson, this is the point where the teacher introduces students to the story that will be brought to life during the lesson. Similarly, if the lesson falls into a curricular area outside of language arts, such as science or social studies, this is where the teacher will discuss the subject of the lesson.
3. Explore story/topic through dramatic activities: While this is only one step in the planning process, exploring the story or topic occupies the bulk of the lesson and usually includes more than one activity.
4. Reflect with participants: Teachers finish a lesson by using a "wrap-up" discussion or closing activity that examines the lesson plan's main goal. Novice classroom teachers should keep in mind that reflection is the synthesizing moment of a lesson when students create meaning out of previous activities. Pressing time constraints at the end of a lesson or not, teachers must incorporate careful reflection at the end of every lesson in order to ensure successful completion of educational goals.
5. Teacher self-reflection: Lifelong learning is one of the great rewards of the teaching profession and reflective practice enables dynamic and thoughtful pedagogy. Whether writing in

---

[4] The author's ideas regarding planning drama lessons has been greatly influenced by Sharon Grady. Dr. Grady writes further about her process in her book, *Drama and Diversity: A Pluralistic Perspective for Educational Drama*, pp. 157–159.

[5] See Michael Rohd's "Warm-Ups" chapter in *Theatre for Community, Conflict, and Dialogue* for further discussion and ideas.

a reflective practitioner journal, or simply taking a few minutes to review outcomes, self-reflection provides the classroom teacher time to consider: What were the most successful parts of the lesson? How did I handle challenging moments during that lesson? How did I prepare for the lesson and how will I plan differently next time? What questions do I still have about the lesson that I will examine for myself next time?

Storytelling: Storytelling involves the creativity of the whole person by stimulating imagination, empathy, and problem-solving skills for the teller and audience alike. When a teacher uses storytelling as a source for classroom activities, a multitude of additional learning outcomes emerge, such as vocal and physical skill enhancement, and student language acquisition. Reading a book out loud to children, or having students read together, is certainly a steadfast method for language arts. However, what are the advantages of teacher as storyteller? Rives Collins and Pamela J. Cooper, co-authors of *Power of Story: Teaching through Storytelling*, summarize the benefits of storytelling and children:

1. Develops appreciation of the beauty and rhythm of language.
2. Increases vocabulary.
3. Refines speaking skills.
4. Improves listening skills.
5. Allows students to interact with adults on a personal level.
6. Enhances writing skills.
7. Sparks an interest in reading.
8. Enhances critical and creative thinking skills.
9. Nourishes students' intuitive side
10. Helps students see literature as a mirror of human experiences.
11. Helps students understand their own and others' cultural heritage.[6]

Some basic and effective storytelling tips for teachers to keep in mind when telling stories include:

1. Practice out loud: Facial muscle memory will help memorization.
2. Incorporate different character voices.
3. Integrate hand gestures.
4. Make eye contact with individuals for 1–3 seconds each.
5. Use descriptive language to bring the story to life for students to imagine in their minds' eye.
6. Condense the story down to five or six major plot points: Students will be able to more readily recall the storyline for later activities if the storyteller keeps a succinct sequence of events.
7. Underscore story with recorded music to enhance theatricality.
8. Plan for dramatic pauses at exciting moments in the story.
9. Use repetition to amplify speech patterns and rhythm of language.
10. Include sound effects and onomatopoeia for dramatic effect.

Historical Influence: Winifred Ward

As one of the most influential figures in American educational drama and the earliest author in the field of creative drama, Winifred Ward's ideas regarding skill development during classroom story dramatization continues to resonate in the twenty-first century classroom. Ward was born in 1884, received a PhD. from the University of Chicago in 1918, and worked as a professor at Northwestern University until she retired in 1950. In the mid-1920s, Ward began one of the most significant university programs in drama and theatre for youth at Northwestern and

---

[6] Collins, Rives, and Pamela J. Cooper. *Power of Story: Teaching through Storytelling* (Long Grove, IL: Waveland Press Inc., 2005), 11–18.

became the original supervisor of creative drama in the Evanston public schools. Ward published four seminal books during her career: *Creative Dramatics* (1930); *Theater for Children* (2nd ed., 1948); *Playmaking with Children* (2nd ed., 1957); *Stories to Dramatize* (1952). In 1944, she was the first committee chair for the Children's Theatre Committee, an organization that continues on today as the American Alliance for Theatre and Education (AATE). Three years after Ward's death in 1975, AATE began presenting, and continues to bestow, the Winifred Ward Memorial Scholarship Award to a leading graduate student in the field of drama and theatre for youth.

Winifred Ward's clear approach to developing creative drama based lessons is dependent on student mastery of certain drama skills, such as pantomime and characterization, before moving on to more complex activities, such as improvisational playmaking. Ward's use of fairy tales, poems, and contemporary narrative offered the source for her story dramatizations and her methods provided the formulas for classroom lesson planning. While Ward insists that the teacher serves as the planner, the implementer, and the guide for the story drama, the teacher must also include carefully planned questions in order for students to connect the drama activities to their own lives.

Ward References: Heinig, Ruth B. (Ed.), *Go Adventuring! A Celebration of Winifred Ward: America's First Lady of Drama for Children* (London: Anchorage Press, 1977).

Rosenberg, Helene S. and Patricia Pinciotti. *Creative Drama and Imagination: Transforming Ideas into Action* (New York, Holt, Rhinehart, and Winston, 1987), 25–29.

Northwestern University Archives, "Winifred Ward Papers," http://files.library.northwestern.edu/findingaids/ward_winifred.pdf (accessed May 31, 2011).

Narrative pantomime: Narrative pantomime is an interactive, educational technique where the teacher narrates character actions for students to simultaneously (and usually, silently) act out. Ruth Beall Heinig, award-winning creative drama specialist and author, explains the advantages of using this technique for the classroom. Heinig writes that narrative pantomimes are:

1. Pragmatic, proficient, and entertaining ways to dramatize excellent literature.
2. Useful for young or beginner groups, as well as valuable for older or more experienced groups
3. Practical for kinesthetic processing of aural information.[7]

Rehearsing a new narrative pantomime will help teachers find appropriate vocal inflections, volume, and pace for children to comfortably follow along. While teachers tend to be the most effective presenter of narrative pantomimes, once children are familiar and comfortable with the technique, the teacher can choose proficient readers to lead the acting, thus making the activity more student-centered.

When choosing, or creating, a narrative pantomime, teachers will find that certain elements contribute to a successful narrative pantomime experience, especially when a teacher first begins incorporating the technique into the classroom.

- One main character, referred to in second person (i.e., "You ride your bicycle. . ."), which all the students can act out at the same time.

- Plenty of playable action, as opposed to inner character thoughts, to keep students actively engaged.

- A teacher reading a narrative pantomime off a paper works well, as long as the teacher is familiar enough with the story to frequently look up off the page in order to monitor the group's comprehension.

[7] Heinig, Ruth Beall, *Creative Drama for the Classroom Teacher* (Upper Saddle River, NJ: Prentice Hall, 1993), 105–106.

- Vocal qualities such as pace, volume, sound effects, and distinct character voices will enhance student understanding of the narrative pantomime's drama world.
- Underscoring the activity with soft music, or using differing classroom lighting, also helps bring the drama world to life during a dynamic narrative pantomime.

Tableau(x): When the word "tableau," a French word that means "picture," is used in a drama context, it means actors in a frozen, silent, group image.[8] It is helpful when giving children directions about this technique to use a synonym such as "photograph" or "snap shot." Including a tableau in a drama lesson purposely slows down the drama, "giving students time to reflect on ideas or capsulize thinking" (Heinig, *Creative Drama for the Classroom Teacher*, p. 164). Sharing small group tableaux in a class provides an opportunity for students observing from outside the tableau to create meaning out of what they see. Teachers may be tempted to use this activity as a "guessing game" for the audience to infer the single "correct" interpretation of the image, but a tableau is appropriately classified as art, and great art provides numerous ways to fittingly interpret intention. Artists always have an *intention* with their creations, although it is the audience's *perception* that carries the most validity in the world of art.

Scene work: Preparing classroom scene work works well in small groups of four to six students. Teachers can help children create scenes by giving the students brief descriptions of scenarios, predetermining titles for the scenes, or suggesting broad topics. Some helpful tips to keep in mind when students are engaging in scene work include:

1. Encouraging children to rehearse before they share with the whole group to help them prepare themselves for performance and lessen performance anxiety.
2. Prompting students to make sure they know how the scene begins and ends. Improvising is always part of this type of scene work, but a definitive beginning and ending will help students feel secure within an agreed-upon structure.
3. Directing students to "face out" or "cheat out" to the audience so their actions and facial expressions can be seen. Teachers can illustrate this point by showing that the front of a person's body and face is a lot more interesting to look at than the back of someone's head.
4. Reminding students to speak loudly and clearly. It can be helpful to tell children to talk to the back of the room when sharing dialogue.
5. Appreciating the efforts of the performers by applauding at the conclusion of a scene.

Sample lesson plan: story drama and language arts: The following lesson plan is an example of how familiar stories can be used as a springboard for various dramatic activities. While this lesson also includes some teacher in role work (see next section), many teachers will find they already possess the improvisational drama skills to play the role outlined in this lesson plan. Teachers are encouraged to employ the lesson plan as it is written before substituting alternate activities for the teacher in role work.

TITLE:	Jack's Giant's Complaint
TARGET AGE GROUP:	Third Grade
GOAL:	To use dramatic activities to develop empathy and cooperation while utilizing language arts skills.

OBJECTIVES:

Students will pantomime characters in a certain situation.
Students will engage in a narrative pantomime.
Students will mold themselves into solo statues.

---

[8] *Tableau* is the singular form of the word, meaning one frozen image. If there is more than one image, an "x" is added at the end of the word: *tableaux*.

Students will embody the character of a Jack or Jacqueline who has been called into a special hearing in the Fairy Land Courthouse.

Students will share the Giants' perspective through scenes.

Students will discuss possible solutions for everyone involved in the situation.

MATERIALS: Music to underscore narrative pantomime, gavel (or robe or other prop) for the leader in role, poster announcing the Fairy Land Courthouse.

PROCEDURE:

1. Warm-up: Relationship Wheel

    a. Group divides into partners; one person is A and the other person is B. All the As form an internal circle and face their partners, who are making an external circle of people.

    b. The pairs are given a relationship and a situation that they must silently pantomime. When the leader calls "SOUND," pairs add dialogue and sound effects.

    c. The external circle of B's steps one person to the right so there are new pairings of As and Bs. Exercise is repeated with new relationships and situations.

    Relationships: Strict teacher and inquisitive student during a math lesson; tired parent and hungry young child in a grocery store; friendly monster and an opera singer playing at the beach; farmer and chicken on a farm.

    (10 min.)

Transition: "So our last relationship was on a farm. Now we're going to work together to create a story that involves a character who lives on a farm."

2. Narrative pantomime.

    Leader narrates the story while the students silently act it out in their own space in the room. *(5 min.)*

You wake up one morning, sit up in bed and stretch. You yawn and think about all you need to do that day on the farm. You get up, quickly make your bed, and go to your barn. You see your cow, Clarabell. You pet your cow. You sit down next to the cow and try to milk her. But there's no milk. You stand up and go to the chicken coop. You check the first nest for eggs. No eggs. You check the second nest for eggs. No eggs. You check a few more nests. You don't find any eggs. You sigh and shake your head. You feel sad that it has been so hard lately to live on the farm. You walk outside your chicken coop and stand still for a moment to think. You remember the beans the man gave you at the market yesterday. He said the beans were magic and would bring you great riches. You reach into your pocket to see if the beans are still there. They are! You throw the beans onto the ground and put a little dirt on top of them. And you watch. And you wait. And you feel impatient, but you continue to wait. And wait. Nothing! You are disappointed. Suddenly a huge beanstalk grows out of the ground straight up into the sky. You look up and try to see the top of the beanstalk. You can't even see where it ends! You carefully try to climb the stalk. It feels very sturdy under you. You start climbing and climbing and climbing some more. The top of the beanstalk ends on top of some clouds that you can stand on. You look around. You see a huge table and a huge chair and a huge nest. You look inside the huge nest and see hundreds of golden eggs! You are so surprised because you've never seen golden eggs. Suddenly, next to you is a large goose. You pet the goose on the head. The goose seems to like it. You pet the goose some more and it lays a golden egg! You think about your farm and how much nicer life would be if you could sell golden eggs. You look at all the golden eggs in the nest and promise yourself you'll just borrow the goose to get some eggs yourself before you bring the goose back. You pick up the goose and start climbing down the bean stalk. You hear a great big loud voice saying, "WHO TOOK MY GOOSE THAT LAYS THE GOLDEN EGGS??!??!!" You climb down the beanstalk as fast as you can. Your feet land on the ground and you look up. Everything is quiet and no one has followed you." FREEZE

Transition: "What is your character feeling right now? What is it thinking?"

3. Statues *(5 min.)*

Students will sculpt themselves into what their character feels at that moment. One half of the group will call out the words they see when they look at the statues, then the groups switch.

Transition: "You have found out that you are not the only Jack or Jacqueline that has gotten a golden goose from a giant. You have been summoned to appear in the county court as part of an official investigation into the recent thefts and vandalization of giant's property.

You'll be getting back into character by bringing your chairs and gathering with the other Jacks and Jacquelines for this special hearing. WHEN YOU SIT DOWN, you will be in role as Jack or Jacqueline. Feel free to discuss this case with the others around you before the judge enters. WHEN YOU SIT DOWN, you will be in role as Jack or Jacqueline."

4. Role Drama session—Preset poster paper, or write on board:

"FAIRY LAND COURTHOUSE—JUDGE GRIMM PRESIDING"
In role, the leader will facilitate the meeting (as Judge Grimm) and begin by calling the session to order:

"Hear ye, hear ye. This session of the Fairy Land Courthouse is now called to order. The honorable Judge Grimm presiding. Allow me to first take role call.
Please everyone raise your left hand. Now repeat after me:

I, Jack or Jacqueline, do solemnly swear to uphold the conduct as outlined in section 6 of the fairy land code.

I will only speak when it is my turn and I will listen to my fellow attendees in the fairy land courthouse. I swear this, on all the happily ever afters in the land, now and forever.

Now, we're here today to address some serious complaints we've been receiving from Giantville. Seems that some young people, all with the name of Jack and Jacqueline have been spotted stealing golden geese from a number of residents in Giantville. You have all been summoned today as part of a special hearing and investigation into this problem, since you are all the Jacks and Jacquelines in the land.

> Why would anyone want to take the giants' golden geese?
> What else could you do to help out your farm?
> Although the giants are upset, they have agreed to help if they can, knowing the problems that are plaguing the farms in the area. Any ideas about how they can help?
> There are so many kind people in Fairy Land. What can they do to help out with the farming problems?

> COURT IS ADJOURNED *(10 min.)*"

Transition: "We have spent some time thinking about this issue from Jack/Jacqueline's perspective. But what about the Giants? How do you think they felt once they realized their geese were gone? How would they react? How would they feel? What would they do?"

5. Tableaux—Each small group creates one tableau that leads them into an active scene. Titles include:

1. The Giants' Revenge

2. The Giants' Happy Ending

3. The Giants Decide to Help

4. Giantville makes a deal with Fairyland

REFLECTION: If you were the judge, what would you do in the situation? What are the solutions that will be acceptable and reasonable for everyone involved?

EXTENSION ACTIVITIES:

Advice to the court—Students write letters/make drawings advising the court about what to do about the problem. Students share letters/drawings in small groups.

Scenes—In small groups, students create scenes showing the solutions they came up with in their letters and drawings.

Dream Sequences—What are the Giants thinking about? Groups create dream sequences of what the giants are dreaming about. First, have a discussion about the strange things that happen in dreams.

What happens in dreams?

What are weird things that happen in dreams different from reality?

Each group will come up with dream sequence scenes to share with the whole group.

Role Drama

Classroom drama uses the elements of the art of theatre. Like any art, it is highly disciplined, not free. Like painters, sculptures, or dancers, the participants are held taut in the discipline of an art form. Thus there are rules of the craft that must be followed if the implicit is to be made explicit. If the classroom drama is going to work so that, as in theater, a slice of life can be taken up and examined. (Betty Jane Wagner, *Dorothy Heathcote: Drama as a Learning Medium*, p. 147.)

A fifth-grade teacher tells the class that the topic of the day's science lesson will look at historically important scientific discoveries. She tells her students that she is bringing in a guest speaker on the topic who is waiting right outside the door. The teacher excuses herself for a moment to bring the guest into the classroom. Once she steps right outside the door into the hallway, the teacher puts on an old-fashioned hat and returns to the classroom holding a beaker. The teacher is "in role" as a research assistant from 1898. She informs the students there has been an explosion in the lab, all work has been destroyed, and she needs their assistance. The teacher refers to the students as Marie Curie's colleagues and asks them to help figure out what Curie was working on in the lab.

This description of a dynamic classroom drama illustrates the possibilities that role drama can bring to a curricular lesson. Role drama, defined by the authors of *Role Drama*, is a technique where "teachers set up imagined situations which students and teachers enter together, *in role*, to explore events, issues, and relationships. What distinguishes role drama from other kinds of drama is that *the teacher takes a role within the drama.*"[9] Role drama is also referred to as "process drama" by many renowned creative drama experts, such as Cecily O'Neill, who focus their definitions on the episodic structure of role drama; a structure that links multiple improvisational activities in order to create a "drama world" where there is no audience, only actors engaged in the same enterprise.[10]

Character work: When children play a character other than themselves, they are developing empathy and critical thinking skills, as well as enhancing their emotional intelligence. Teachers' use of characters in the classroom helps engage students in a lesson; however, this type of role work is best suited for teachers who enjoy acting and improvisation. Before teachers attempt to engage in any type of character work in the classroom, they should keep drama expert Nellie McCaslin's word of warning in mind: "A popular method may not be for you, whereas you may have devised a strategy that works well in your situation" (p. 277).

In order for students to feel successful when playing a character, the teacher must first lead students through activities to help them prepare to improvise in role. Scaffolding is a key consideration when preparing students to participate in a role drama. Teachers should design preparation activities to help students warm-up the tools of the actor with specific attention to the characters the teacher will ask the students to portray later in the lesson. Revisiting the premise of utilizing the "tools of the actor" is helpful when planning activities:

- *Warming up the actor's **mind** engages student **creativity:*** Writing activities will give students time to imagine dialogue before they are required to say something in role.

---

[9] Tarlington, Carole and Patrick Verriour. *Role Drama* (Portsmouth, NH: Heinemann, 1991), 9.

[10] O'Neill, Cecily. *Drama Worlds: A Framework for Process Drama* (Portsmouth, NH: Heinemann, 1995), xvi.

- *Warming up the actor's **body** engages students **physically:*** Whole-group pantomime activities provide an opportunity for students to embody a character before they are asked to play their character in a role drama setting, or small group scenes.
- *Warming up the actor's **voice** engages students **verbally:*** Adding dialogue to an ongoing silent pantomime allows students to think about improvised lines as they are acting before speaking them aloud.

Mantle of the Expert: "Mantle of the Expert" is a technique credited to Dorothy Heathcote (see "Historical Influence"). What makes Mantle of the Expert different from a traditional classroom role drama is the *status of the characters.* In other words, *students must be in roles as experts whereas the teacher plays the role of a novice* in order for the activity to be a true Mantle of the Expert experience (i.e., someone who needs the experts' help).

Even within the frame of a fictional drama world, teachers may be reticent to try a technique where they intentionally relinquish the power position in their classroom. However, there are several advantages for teachers who use Mantle of The Expert during a curricular lesson:

1. Empowering students
2. Assessing student knowledge
3. Encouraging cooperative, student-centered learning

Even if a teacher feels she is lacking the experience to convincingly portray a character, the teacher's commitment to the role, the reality of the drama context she has created, and her use of questioning will contribute to a meaningful educational experience for her students. The types of questions a teacher chooses to ask at any moment in the classroom is essential to student understanding and self-confidence. National award winning authors Norah Morgan and Juliana Saxton present six types of questioning based on Bloom's Taxonomy of Educational Objectives in their book, *Asking Better Questions.* Teachers will want to consider the six types of questioning before they decide whether the questions will prompt remembering, understanding, solving, reasoning, creating, or judging information.[11] Dorothy Heathcote, a prominent creative drama expert, believes questioning is the most important tool for longer drama sessions. Author of *Dorothy Heathcote: Drama as a Learning Medium,* Betty Jane Wagner notes that Heathcote's use of questioning, combined with a wide range of nonverbal signals and spoken contributions, enables Heathcote "to get the class involved in, committed to, and finally reflective about a drama that explores significant human experience" (p. 60).

Historical influence: Dorothy Heathcote

Since the 1970s, American drama educators have been greatly influenced by the work and ideas of British educator, Dorothy Heathcote (b. 1926–d. 2011). Heathcote only stayed in school until the age of 14, then worked for five years in a wool mill when she was finally encouraged to return to school and become an actress. Her large stature kept her from playing age appropriate stage roles and Heathcote turned to teaching after the urgings of a university instructor. Although she had no formal education or qualifications to become a teacher, Heathcote's reputation for her innovative teaching methods grew after she became a tutor in 1951. In 1964, Heathcote began teaching university courses, then started lecturing abroad, most notably on her practices of "Mantle of the Expert," "rolling role" (a team-teaching model where different teachers take on characters at different times that all exist in one drama world or context), and "commission models" (school communities working to create a published product for a real or make believe client). Heathcote's unique techniques place emphasis on teachers and students playing characters as they explore dramatic tension provided by real-world situations.

---

[11] Morgan, Norah and Juliana Saxton. *Asking Better Questions* (Portland, OR: Pembroke, 2006), 20–24.

Heathcote References Heathcote, Dorothy and Gavin Bolton. _Drama for Learning: Dorothy Heathcote's Mantle of the Expert Approach to Education_ (Portsmouth, NH: Heinemann, 1994).

Mantle of the Expert.com Web Site. "Dorothy Heathcote." http://www.mantleoftheexpert .com/community/about-us/dorothy-heathcote/ (accessed May 31, 2011).

New York University-Steinhardt School Web Site. "Educational Theatre Faculty: Dorothy Heathcote." http://steinhardt.nyu.edu/music/edtheatre/people/faculty/heathcote (accessed May 31, 2011).

Name: _____

DISCUSSION QUESTIONS

Please type your responses to each question on a separate hard copy, OR legibly hand write directly on this page (use back of sheet as needed) and hand in. Each response needs to be *at least* 3 sentences long (3 sentences = minimum requirement for a paragraph)

1. Find a piece of children's literature that has plenty of playable action. Write the storyline into a narrative pantomime and hand in as part of this response. Test out your activity on a classmate or friend. How would you define the most successful moments of your narrative pantomime? How would you incorporate your narrative pantomime into a language arts curriculum? What state or national educational standards are you directly fulfilling with this technique?

2. Consider the sample lesson plan presented in this section. Which tools of the actor are used in the **engagement** activity? How will the engagement activity help prepare students for success during later activities? Write two more reflection questions for the end of the lesson that will help students synthesize the lesson plan's activities and explore the main goal.

3. What is your most dominant learning style (i.e., spatial, kinesthetic)? Support your choice with examples. How can you incorporate your own learning style for self-reflection? What is your plan for integrating personal self-reflection for your teaching?

4. Visualize a moment when your principal has asked you why you use character work in your classroom. How will you explain the advantages of using this technique for educational purposes?

5. Compare Winifred Ward's contributions to the creative drama field to Dorothy Heathcote's techniques. What are the similarities between Ward and Heathcote? What are the differences? Which method lines up with your teaching style and why?

CREATING ORIGINAL PRODUCTIONS WITH STUDENTS

Most people have memories of participating in school plays as children. Maybe you, the reader, have your own memories. Did you play a part during your fifth-grade classroom production of "Alice in Wonderland?" Do you remember standing on stage as a cloud for your kindergarten's presentation at the school assembly? Perhaps you still remember the poem you recited in front of your class for Arbor Day? Memorable childhood performance experiences not only help develop public speaking skills, but they also serve as a life-long reminder of the empowering feelings of self-worth that actors experience during live performance. The national theater standards establish the importance of teaching and appreciating theater as a performing art form.[12] The Kennedy Center, located in Washington, DC, publishes national standards for arts education, while individual states create their own set of arts education standards. For national theater standards, as well as national standards for other arts, see www.artsedge.kennedy-center.org/educators/standards.

Unfortunately, some young acting memories may be tarnished with negative experiences of stage fright and performance anxiety. Instead of reliving cherished memories when you think back to your elementary school productions, you may be the student who forgot all their lines in front of the whole auditorium. Or, after weeks of intense rehearsal, you were the fourth grader who accidentally exited the stage before your big monologue and was dragged back on the stage by your teacher, as you heard the laughter of a group of fifth graders. These are memorable experiences for all the wrong reasons. Many times, teachers insist on a certain type of performance experience without considering the individuals within the class. As creative drama expert Ruth Beall Heinig writes, "[. . .] sharing [with an audience] should be the collective desire of the group rather than being imposed by [the teacher]" (p. 121).

The theatre material discussed thus far in this text has shown how drama can be used as a learning medium, where "the teacher is using these procedures to reach certain extrinsic goals: to convey knowledge, arouse interest, solve problems, and change attitudes" (McCaslin, p. 261). However, creative drama techniques can also be used to teach about theatre as an art form during units when the classroom community intends to create a production. As long as venues for elementary school productions are "confined to school assemblies, where a sympathetic invited audience will view the product with knowledge of the process," then children will not be expected to use certain acting skills "until their bodies and voices have matured" (McCaslin, p. 261). Once the classroom drama focus has moved from the student learning process to preparing for a production, then the creative drama work has relocated into the realm of theatre.

This section will show you how to:

- Incorporate activities to produce original plays with young people.
- Enhance theatrical elements within the confines of school performing spaces.
- Set up successful, student-centered, unique performance experiences for young students.

Activities for Student-Generated Work

The most obvious advantage for using student-generated pieces is the decrease in performance anxiety. Since the students create the material themselves, they are more likely to remember sequence of events and cue lines. There is also opportunity for students to enter the performance in Vygotsky's Zone of Actual Development (ZAD) and help one another move into Zone of Proximal Development (ZPD). For instance, "if some students are hesitant with dialogue, they can still

---

[12] At time of publication, the National Theatre Arts Standards were still under review in draft form.

participate in the playing, and those who are ready for improvising can add it" (Heinig, p. 121). Some activity ideas for teachers to try when creating new performance pieces include:

1. Use narrative pantomimes for plays. Allowing actors a certain amount of improvisational dialogue or "stage business" within the set structure of the storyline's action can decrease the fear of getting the lines "wrong." "Fear of forgetting lines," Heinig writes about as one of the biggest concerns when performing a play, "can be eliminated since these plays go on as long as the narrating and pantomiming continue."
2. Incorporate multiple tableaux for pivotal narrative points, and then underscore transitions with music.
3. Use a familiar story as a source and allow students to create alternate endings.
4. Combine pop culture and school curriculum: Parody a familiar movie or television show.
    a. Insert characters from a book the class is reading.
    b. Insert historical figures from a period the class is studying.
    c. Utilize a curricular concept (i.e., math measurements, science concepts) as part of a real-life conflict within the dramatic context.

Student-generated work allows another opportunity for the classroom teacher to structure student-centered activities that mold to students' strengths and safely challenges their comfort zones in their learning environment. Students feel a sense of empowerment when they hear their words and ideas in performance.

Teacher as Director and Designer: Performance choices

Whether a play comes alive in a second-grade classroom or on the stage of a Broadway theater, thoughtful adherence to certain dramatic principles will keep audiences engaged in the performance. Oscar Brockett and Robert J. Ball, authors of the tenth edition of *The Essential Theatre*, cite these elements as:

- The script.
- The physical and mental capacities of the actors.
- The performance space or stage, and inclusion of any scenery or props.
- Costumes and/or makeup.
- Lighting.
- Sound.[13]

When a classroom teacher first begins crafting original scripts with his or her students, a "climactic plot structure" provides the most recognizable series of events for the audience. Once teachers are more comfortable creating original performance pieces with children, or if the teacher already possesses experience with various dramatic constructs, there are a number of exciting options for less linear, conservative plot formations.[14] Teachers should first clarify beginning, middle, and end moments for the flow of the story. Boundaries, such as a set story form established by the teacher, will help children feel secure enough to improvise within a structure. Second, in terms of content, a complete piece must have an obvious dilemma or conflict in order for characters to present a satisfying resolution. Finally, teachers need to consider how the play unifies setting, characterization, and action in order to create a coherent product.

---

[13] Brockett, Oscar G. and Robert J. Ball, *The Essential Theatre* (Boston: Wadsworth, 2011).
[14] Until the classroom teacher feels comfortable experimenting with other structures, the author suggests sticking with a traditional "rising action, climax, falling action" plot construction.

SAMPLE IDEA FOR A CULMINATING INTEGRATIVE ARTS PERFORMANCE

MUSIC, ART, THEATRE FOR ELEMENTARY EDUCATION—FINAL PROJECT

Create a 10–15-minute presentation on a selected topic.

- First, choose a theme or "big idea" from the list below, or come up with your own theme.

Fear	Protest	Memory
Identity	Compassion	Place
Ritual/celebration	Aging	Loss
Interdependence	Transformation	Change
Spirituality	Community	Time
Relationships	Nature	Power
Fantasy/reality	Suffering	Conflict
Diversity	Stories	Journey
Paradox	Systems	Materialism/Consumption
Heroes		

- Second, select a subject area (i.e. Language Arts, Science, Social Studies, Math, etc.).
- Third, select a grade level.
- Finally, choose a Grade Level Content Standard or Common Core Standard.

For example. . .

Theme: Journey

Subject: Math

Grade Level: Fourth

Common Core Standard (Michigan): CCSS.Math.Content.4.MD.A.2 Use the four operations to solve word problems involving distances, intervals of time, liquid volumes, masses of objects, and money, including problems involving simple fractions or decimals, and problems that require expressing measurements given in a larger unit in terms of a smaller unit. Represent measurement quantities using diagrams such as number line diagrams that feature a measurement scale.

Brief Description of Presentation: The presentation will focus on a family planning a vacation. It must figure out how to measure the distances the family will travel between locations, the intervals of time they will spend at their destinations, and the amount of money they will be spending on the journey.

PRESENTATION REQUIREMENTS: The 10–15-minute performance must include the following elements from Music, Art, and Theatre disciplines.

MUSIC: Two piggyback songs where every performer sings and/or plays musical accompaniment; at least two musical recordings.

ART: Character masks or artifact (props, etc.) with convincing visual characterization, craftsmanship, and user-friendly problem solving. Performance must integrate the theme and art production meaningfully and aesthetically.

THEATRE: Every participant must perform as at least one character, and/or the narrator, while paying attention to vocal volume, articulation, inflection, rate, and pitch. Final piece must be obviously well prepared and memorized; at least one tableau(x); a storyline with an obvious conflict that appropriately ties into theme; at least one dramatic activity at the end of the performance where audience reflects directly on the main objective of the performance and interactively demonstrates their understanding of the main goal of the performance.

Devising a classroom performance requires the teacher to consider all the same theatrical resources used by a director. According to Aristotle, spectacle is one of the main components of drama. In a traditional theatre performance, visual elements, such as lighting and scenery, add to a production's sense of spectacle. With a little creativity, teachers can create their own unique sense of spectacle during their classroom drama lessons. Even limited by a classroom space, teachers can get creative with their presentation choices. Turning out some of the overhead lights in a classroom, hanging strands of lights, adding in simple sound effects, playing background music, and including indicative costume pieces for different characters, enhances the overall theatricality during an exciting educational experience.

A final consideration for classroom communities creating a production: a performance endeavor will best be served by a teacher who has some background in theatre. The process of leading creative drama activities in a classroom will help prepare students to perform and teachers to direct, although it is no substitute for production experience. Creative drama and children's theatre expert Nellie McCaslin writes:

> The transition from classroom to stage should come easily and naturally to the group that has spent many hours in improvisation; for boys and girls who have played together informally for some time, the result is more likely to be one of "sharing" than "showing," and to this end the teacher should be able to help the players achieve their goal—successful communication with the audience.[15]

Exposure to live theatrical events will also help prime children and teachers for performance. Professional children's theaters and touring companies exist across the United States. The American Alliance for Theatre and Education (AATE) and Theatre for Young Audiences (TYA) USA are two professional organizations that can help classroom teachers locate developmentally appropriate local children's theatre performances.[16]

Historical influence: Nellie McCaslin

Dr. Nellie McCaslin (1914–2005) and her classic textbook *Creative Drama in the Classroom and Beyond* has guided generations of students in the field of children's theatre and creative drama. During her seven decades of teaching and writing at institutions such as Mills College, Columbia University, and New York University, McCaslin also presented and lectured internationally about the creative and intellectual power of theatre arts education and arts integration. Her publications include *Theatre for Children in the United States: A History* (1971), *Children and Drama* (1975), and *Theatre for Young Audiences* (1978), as well as eight editions of *Creative Drama in the Classroom and Beyond* (2006) that were revised over a span of 35 years. Actively creating new plays and performing right up to her death at the age of 90, McCaslin capped her career by putting forth six enduring insights about the field of drama and theatre for youth:

1. Children can and do have an aesthetic experience in both a creative drama class and formal theatre.

---

[15] McCaslin, Nellie. *Creative Drama in the Classroom and Beyond* (Boston: Pearson Education Inc., 2006), 304.
[16] For more information, visit the AATE website at www.aate.com and the TYA USA website at www.assitej-usa.org.

2. Theatre begins in play, from which with guidance it develops a dramatic structure of its own (creative drama).
3. Imagination is the magic force for both players and audience.
4. The aesthetic distance between the art and the child audience can disappear and immediately be restored by the child, unlike his or her adult counterpart.
5. The best theatre imparts information and understanding without a hidden agenda.
6. Finally, creative drama and theatre, process and product, share the same three objectives [. . .]. Both offer an aesthetic encounter, an educational experience, and a social opportunity unique among the arts.[17]

McCaslin's published work will define her for years to come as an author and educator with passion and in-depth understanding of the relationship between creative drama and children's theatre.

McCaslin References Fox, Margalita, "Nellie McCaslin, Professor and Children's Theater Authority, Dies at 90." *New York Times*-Online Edition, March 12, 2005. http://www.nytimes.com/2005/03/12/theater/12mccaslin.html. (accessed May 31, 2011).

Martin-Smith, Alistair, "A Personal Tribute to Nellie McCaslin," 20 August 1914-28 February 2005 The Journal of Aesthetic Education, 39 (4), (Winter 2005:1–2).

Published by University of Illinois Press.

McCaslin, Nellie. *Creative Drama in the Classroom and Beyond* (Boston: Pearson Education Inc., 2006).

---

[17] McCaslin, Nellie. "Seeking the Aesthetic in Creative Drama and Theatre for Young Audiences," *The Journal of Aesthetic Education*, Volume 39, Number 4, Winter 2005, pp. 12–19.

Name: _____

DISCUSSION QUESTIONS

Please type your responses to each question on a separate hard copy, OR legibly hand write directly on this page (use back of sheet as needed) and hand in. Each response needs to be at least 3 sentences long (3 sentences = minimum requirement for a paragraph)

1. Describe a memorable theatrical performance experience from your childhood. Why was it memorable? What did you learn from the experience? How can you use your memory to craft positive performance experiences for your students?

2. Visualize yourself as a teacher whose students have just been asked to create an original, end of-the-school-year performance for a play titled, "The Most Important Thing We Learned in School This Year." Which two or three activities described in the Theatre section of this book will you use with your students? Discuss why you chose these particular activities for your classroom.

3. Explain, in your own words, the difference between a traditional theatrical performance and using drama as a teaching tool in the classroom.

4. Review Nellie McCaslin's final six points. Which one resonates with you the most and why? Support your response with a personal experience and/or citations from this book.

THEATRE SECTION RESOURCES AND REFERENCES

Brockett, Oscar G. and Robert J. Ball. *The Essential Theatre* (Boston: Wadsworth, Cengage Learning, 2011).

Collins, Rives and Pamela J. Cooper. *The Power of the Story: Teaching through Storytelling* (Long Grove, IL: Waveland Press Inc., 2005).

Fennessey, Sharon M. *History in the Spotlight: Creative Drama and Theatre Practices for the Social Studies Classroom* (Portsmouth, NH: Heinemann, 2000).

Gardner, Howard. *Intelligence Reframed: Multiple Intelligences for the 21st Century* (New York: Basic Books, 1999).

Goldberg, Merryl. *Arts Integration: Teaching Subject Matter through the Arts in Multicultural Settings* (Boston: Pearson Education Inc., 2012).

Goldberg, Moses. *Children's Theatre: A Philosophy and a Method* (Englewood Cliffs, NJ: Prentice-Hall Inc., 1974).

Goleman, Daniel. *Emotional Intelligence: Why it can matter more than IQ* (New York: Bantam Books, 1995).

Grady, Sharon. *Drama and Diversity: A Pluralistic Perspective for Educational Drama* (Portsmouth, NH: Heinemann, 2000).

Heinig, Ruth Beall. *Improvisation with Favorite Tales: Integrating Drama into the Reading/Writing Classroom* (Portsmouth, NH: Heinemann, 1992).

Heinig, Ruth Beall. *Creative Drama for the Classroom Teacher* (Upper Saddle River, NJ: Prentice-Hall Inc., 1993).

Kelner, Lenore Blank. *The Creative Classroom: A Guide for Using Creative Drama in the Classroom, PreK-6* (Portsmouth, NH: Heinemann, 1993).

Kelner, Lenore Blank and Rosalind M. Flynn. *A Dramatic Approach to Reading Comprehension: Strategies and Activities for Classroom Teachers* (Portsmouth, NH: Heinemann, 2006).

Mandell, Jane and Jennifer Lynn Wolf. *Acting, Learning, & Change: Creating Original Plays with Adolescents* (Portsmouth, NH: Heinemann, 2003).

McCaslin, Nellie. *Creative Drama in the Classroom and Beyond* (Boston: Pearson Education, Inc., 2006).

McDonald, Nan L. *Handbook for K-8 Arts Integration: Purposeful Planning across the Curriculum* (Boston: Pearson Education, Inc., 2010).

Morgan, Norah and Juliana Saxton. *Asking Better Questions* (Markham: Pembroke Publishers Limited, 2006).

O'Neill, Cecily. *Drama Worlds: A Framework for Process Drama* (Portsmouth, NH: Heinemann, 1995).

O'Neill, Cecily and Alan Lambert. *Drama Structures: A Practical Handbook for Teachers* (Portsmouth, NH: Heinemann, 1994).

Peterson, Lenka and Dan O'Connor. *Kids Take the Stage: Helping Young People Discover the Creative Outlet of Theater* (New York: Back Stage Books, 1997).

Powell, Mary Clare and Vivien Marcow Speiser (Eds). *The Arts, Education, and Social Change: Little Signs of Hope* (New York: Peter Lang Publishing Inc., 2005).

Rohd, Michael. *Hope is Vital: Theatre for Community, Conflict, & Dialogue* (Portsmouth, NH: Heinemann, 1998).

Rooyackers, Paul. *101 Dance Games for Children: Fun and Creativity with Movement* (Alameda, CA: Hunter House Inc., 1995).

Salazar, Laura Gardner. *Making Performance Art* (Charlottesville, VA: New Plays Incorporated, 1999).

Saldaña, Johnny. *Drama of Color: Improvisation with Multiethnic Folklore* (Portsmouth, NH: Heinemann, 1995).

Schneider, Jenifer Jasinski, Thomas P. Crumpler and Theresa Rogers (Eds). *Process Drama and Multiple Literacies: Addressing Social, Cultural, and Ethical Issues* (Portsmouth, NH: Heinemann, 2006).

Spolin, Viola. *Theater Games for the Classroom: A Teacher's Handbook* (Evanston, IL: Northwestern University Press, 1986).

Tarlington, Carole and Patrick Verriour. *Role Drama* (Portsmouth, NH: Pembroke Publishers Limited, 1991).

Wagner, Betty Jane. *Dorothy Heathcote: Drama as a Learning Medium* (London: Hutchinson & Co. Ltd., 1979).

Wagner, Betty Jane (Ed). *Building Moral Communities Through Educational Drama* (Stamford, CT: Ablex Publishing Corporation, 1999).

Wainscott, Ronald and Kathy Fletcher. *Theatre: Collaborative Acts* (Boston: Pearson Education Inc., 2009).

Wilhelm, Jeffrey D. *Action Strategies for Deepening Comprehension* (New York: Scholastic Inc., 2002).

Wilhelm, Jeffrey D. and Brian Edmiston. *Imagining to Learn: Inquiry, Ethics, and Integration through Drama* (Portsmouth, NH: Heinemann, 1998).